# Student Guide to Accompany

# EDUCATIONAL RESEARCH
## Competencies for Analysis and Application

## Fifth Edition

Prepared by

L.R. Gay
Florida International University

Merrill, an imprint of Prentice Hall
Englewood Cliffs, New Jersey Columbus, Ohio

Cover image: P. Degginger/H. Armstrong Roberts
Editor: Kevin M. Davis
Developmental Editor: Carol S. Sykes
Production Editor: Julie Anderson Tober
Cover Designer: Julia Zonneveld Van Hook
Production Manager: Patricia A. Tonneman

A Simon & Schuster Company
Englewood Cliffs, New Jersey 07632



Printed in the United States of America

9 8 7 6 5

ISBN: 0-13-502337-8

Prentice-Hall International (UK) Limited, *London*
Prentice-Hall of Australia Pty. Limited, *Sydney*
Prentice-Hall Canada Inc., *Toronto*
Prentice-Hall Hispanoamericana, S. A., *Mexico*
Prentice-Hall of India Private Limited, *New Delhi*
Prentice-Hall of Japan, Inc., *Tokyo*
Simon & Schuster Asia Pte. Ltd., *Singapore*
Editora Prentice-Hall do Brasil, Ltda., *Rio de Janeiro*

CONTENTS

# PART ONE

## INTRODUCTION

**Task 1-A**

**Given a reprint of a research study, identify and briefly state:**

**a) the problem (purpose of the study),**
**b) the procedures,**
**c) the method of analysis, and**
**d) the major conclusion.**

**Beginning on the next page, research reports are reprinted. Following each reprint, spaces are provided for listing the components required by Task 1-A. As a self-test, after you have studied Part One, select at least two of the reprints (any two that look interesting to you) and see if you can identify the components. If your responses match the Suggested Responses in the back of this book, you are ready for Task 1-A. If your responses differ greatly from the Suggested Responses, study the articles again until you see why you were in error and then select two other articles and repeat the process. If by some chance you incorrectly identify the components of all five research reports, see your instructor.**

# Reading Time in School: Effect on Fourth Graders' Performance on a Criterion-Referenced Comprehension Test

**D. RAY REUTZEL**
**PAUL M. HOLLINGSWORTH**
**Brigham Young University**

ABSTRACT **This study explored the effect of time spent reading versus time spent learning and practicing specific reading comprehension skills as measured by criterion-referenced reading comprehension skill test (CRTs) scores. This educational question is important because many teachers and administrators are reticent to allocate more instructional time to sustained reading of connected text for fear of declining performance on locally administered CRTs. Sixty-one 4th graders were randomly assigned to three different treatment conditions: (a) reading only, (b) reading/skill instruction, and (c) skill instruction only. All the students received 30 min per day of basal reading instruction in their intact classrooms. None of the skills taught in the skill groups were taught during this time. For the remaining 30 min of the 60-min reading period, the students moved to their assigned conditions. Students in the reading-only group read books of their own choosing for 30 min each day for 30 days. Students in the skills-only group received skill instruction and practice on four reading comprehension skills for 30 min each day. Students in the combined reading/skill instruction group read books of their own choosing each day for 15 min and received skill lessons on the same four reading comprehension skill instructed in the skills-only group for the remaining 15 min each day. Results indicated significant pre- to posttest growth for all groups for each of the four reading comprehension skills. However, no differences were found among the three treatment conditions following the 30-day treatment period. The findings tend to argue for increasing time spent reading rather than spending time practicing specific reading skills for the fourth-grade students because reading books produced equivalent gains from pre- to posttest conditions on the CRTs for the four comprehension skills instructed and measured.**

Each day in school a significant part of classroom instructional time, typically 70 min, is allocated for reading instruction. Despite that fact, evidence suggests that children spend only 7–8 min of allocated reading instructional time *reading* in the primary grades and only 15 min per day *reading* in the intermediate grades. Fisher, Berliner, Filby, Marliave, Cohen, Dishaw, and Moore (1978) and Anderson, Hiebert, Scott, and Wilkinson (1985) indicate that students spend the bulk of allocated reading instructional time, up to 70%, engaged in independent seatwork completing worksheets, skill sheets, and ditto papers. According to publishers, the demand for workbook and skill sheet activities has become so widespread that it has created an insatiable need for seatwork and workbook activity pages despite the fact that worksheet activities require only perfunctory levels of reading practice (Anderson, Hiebert, Scott, & Wilkinson, 1985, p. 74; Jachym, Allington, & Broikou, 1989; Osborn, 1984, 1985).

The current emphasis on learning to read by using worksheets and skill sheets continues in spite of the fact that research has documented sharp increases in reading achievement scores associated with regular and sustained reading in and out of school (Anderson, Wilson, & Fielding, 1988; Leinhardt, Zigmond, & Cooley, 1981). Time spent reading outside of school is no greater than time spent reading in school. Additionally, Fielding, Wilson, and Anderson (1986) reported that 50% of children read books 4 min per day or less outside of school. In light of the data, one is prompted to ask why so little time in school is allocated for engaging children in sustained and regular reading.

Morrow (1986) assessed teachers', principals', and parents' attitudes toward promoting voluntary reading in school by asking them to rank four reading activities: comprehension instruction, word recognition instruction,

*Address correspondence to Paul M. Hollingsworth, College of Education, Department of Elementary Education, 215 McKay Building, Brigham Young University, Provo, UT 84602.*

voluntary reading, and study skill instruction. With respect to improving standardized reading achievement test scores, those individuals ranked voluntary reading as least important. Also, voluntary reading was ranked last among the four reading activities in overall importance. Although teachers, principals, and parents generally rated voluntary reading as an important part of the reading instructional program, time spent engaged in learning and mastering basic reading skills was deemed to be of greater importance than time spent reading.

At least three potential explanations exist for Morrow's (1986) findings. The first explanation is related to instructional traditions. The teaching of reading as a skill has become the norm—what is expected. Shannon (1983) and Farr, Tulley, and Powell (1987) found that the published basal and its attendant list of skills has become, in the minds of most teachers and administrators, *the* reading program. For example, Durkin's (1984) and Mason's (1983) examinations of classroom reading instruction determined that teachers seldom, if ever, neglected skill instruction or the accompanying seatwork. In contrast, background building, language extension, and sustained reading activities were typically overlooked or explained away by teachers as relatively unimportant. In a sense, the act of reading itself has been displaced in large measure by published instructional programs and skill lists (Goodman, Shannon, Freeman, & Murphy, 1988; Shannon, 1989).

A second explanation for Morrow's (1986) findings is related to state- and district-mandated reading curricula. Many state and district reading curricula have mandated a sequence of basic reading skills to be taught, mastered, and tested, thus prolonging the teaching of reading as a skill rather than as reading (Shannon, 1989).

A third potential explanation for Morrow's (1986) findings regarding the importance of voluntary reading in the schools may focus on a generalized concern over a potential decline in performance on district-mandated tests of reading skills (Goodman, Shannon, Freeman, & Murphy, 1988; Shannon, 1989). Stern and Shavelson (1983) and Mosenthal (1989) indicate that teachers and administrators feel pressured to use classroom time for skill development because they believe such practices will help children achieve higher test scores.

Although some recent evidence has shown that sustained reading has a beneficial effect on standardized reading achievement test scores (Anderson, Wilson, & Fielding, 1988), no research has investigated the potential impact that a program of regular and sustained reading may have on criterion-referenced skill test scores. Research investigating that question is of particular significance because criterion-referenced test scores are often thought to be a much more immediate and specific measure of instructional effectiveness and student progress through a state- or district-mandated reading curriculum than are standardized achievement tests. In fact, the threat of declining criterion-referenced test scores is as much a threat to teachers, administrators, and parents as is the potential decline of standardized reading achievement test scores (Goodman, Shannon, Freeman, & Murphy, 1988). More important, criterion-referenced reading test scores are often used by teachers, principals, and administrators in making decisions about important changes in classroom practices and student performance (Shannon, 1989).

Additional support for a study of the effect of time spent reading in school on criterion-referenced reading skill test scores can be found in the writings of Rosenshine (1980), who suggested an experiment involving teaching and measuring several reading comprehension skills with the following recommendation: ". . . another factor could be introduced to see whether time spent in reading itself is as effective as time spent on reading [skill] exercises" (p. 552).

Thus, our study was designed to explore the impact that a regular and sustained self-selected reading program may have on a selected set of reading skills measured by a criterion-referenced reading skill test. Without sufficient evidence to support allocating more time spent reading each day in schools, one may reasonably expect that teachers and administrators will remain reticent to replace current reading instructional practices with additional time spent reading. Therefore, the answer to our research question is of particular practical importance for administrative and classroom decision making.

## Procedure

### *Subjects*

Our sample contained 61 fourth-grade students attending a middle- to lower class suburban elementary school located in the Rocky Mountain region. We selected fourth-grade students for this study for two reasons. First, reading comprehension instruction tends to become more pronounced than decoding instruction in the intermediate grades. Second, teachers and publishers assume that children in the fourth grade have developed sufficient reading skills to shift the emphasis away from decoding instruction or learning to read to comprehension instruction or reading to learn. Evidence for that assumption can be found in classroom practice, in state and district curriculum guides, and in basal readers (Anderson, Hiebert, Scott, & Wilkinson, 1985). The subjects in this study represented a broad array of achievement levels and a few minority students, mainly Hispanic.

### *Design*

We used a pretest-posttest comparison group design for this study. The data for the study were analyzed using four separate analyses of covariance. We used a table of random numbers to randomly assign students to three comparison groups (reading only, $n = 20$; skills only, $n = 21$; reading/skills comparison group, $n = 20$).

The three groups of students were distributed randomly among six different teachers—three classroom teachers and three graduate students who were trained to participate in this experiment. Each teacher/graduate student was randomly assigned to one of the three treatment conditions, resulting in six treatment groups of about 10–11 students, two groups for each of the three treatment conditions. Because of random assignment, students moved from their intact classrooms to other classrooms in the school or the media center for the three reading-treatment conditions.

The covariate in each of the four separate analyses of covariance (ANCOVA) was the appropriate pretest score on a criterion-referenced reading comprehension skill test. To assess the effectiveness of the random assignment of subjects to treatments, we used analysis of variance (ANOVA) to analyze fall-semester scores on the California Test of Basic Skills (CTBS) Reading Comprehension subtest, given 1 month prior to the experiment. There was no significant difference among the treatment groups at the onset of instruction according to their measured reading achievement scores on the CTBS, $F(2, 59) = .49$, $p > .05$. A subsequent multiple analysis of variance (MANOVA) of the four reading comprehension skill subtest scores for the three treatment groups also showed no difference among the three treatment groups at the outset of the study, $F(8, 110) = 1.09$, $\lambda = .86$, $p > .38$.

*Instrumentation*

The two instruments for the study consisted of the comprehension subtest of a standardized achievement test, the CTBS and a researcher-designed Specific Comprehension Skills Test (SCST). The CTBS comprehension subtest was used to determine the initial equivalency of the three treatment groups. We developed the SCST by using items taken from the Barnell Loft Specific Skills Series. The SCST is composed of one pretest and one posttest form, with items representing each of the following four specific reading comprehension skill areas: (a) noting details, (b) drawing conclusions, (c) finding the sequence, and (d) determining main ideas. The preceding four reading comprehension skills were selected because they form the core of reading comprehension skills typically taught and assessed in public schools and in published reading materials (Durkin, 1981; Rosenshine, 1980). Furthermore, the number and types of reading skills selected for instruction, practice, and assessment in our study were limited to only four reading comprehension skills. Although we recognized that many other reading skills involving decoding or study skills could have been selected for instruction and assessment in this study, teachers and principals in Morrow's (1986) study ranked comprehension skills as most important. We felt that the study should examine those reading skills that were ranked highest and were of most importance to teachers, principals, and parents. Furthermore, the grade level of the subjects chosen for this study seemed to logically support the selection of reading comprehension skills rather than decoding skills.

The pretest and posttest forms of the SCST were composed of four sections, one section for each of the four comprehension skills listed above. Both the pre- and posttest SCST used a multiple-choice format with 12 items for noting details, 15 items for drawing conclusions, 24 items for finding the sequence, and 15 items for determining the main ideas. The subsections of the SCST forms were not labeled; therefore, the subjects taking the tests did not know which specific skills were being tested in each section. The Specific Comprehension Skills Test was used to determine students' gains in selected reading comprehension skills typically taught and assessed in public schools.

To validate and assess reliability, we administered the Specific Comprehension Skill Test forms to a population of 25 fourth-grade students in another local school. Two weeks later, the same tests were administered again to determine test-retest coefficients of stability for the SCST. The results indicated coefficients of stability ranging from .80–.92 for the four skills tested (noting details = .81, drawing conclusions = .80, finding the sequence = .85, and determining the main idea = .92). The same group of fourth-grade students was given the comprehension subtest of the Gates-MacGinitie Reading Survey, Level D, Second Edition. The scores were correlated with the section scores on the SCST to establish concurrent validity coefficients. The coefficients were as follows: noting details = .75; drawing conclusions = .82; finding the sequence = .77; and determining the main idea = .81. Because two forms of the SCST were used (pre- and posttests), we calculated an alternate-forms reliability for the two tests. The results revealed coefficients of equivalency ranging from .79 to .87.

*Treatments*

The six teachers involved in this study agreed to participate in our special teacher training sessions prior to and during the experiment. The teachers were told not to discuss their teaching techniques or lessons with each other or with anyone else during the duration of the experiment. Each teacher agreed to comply with our request.

The skills-only teachers were provided with materials and 30 lessons for planning and implementing the instructional procedures for their specific skill treatments. The researchers modeled how to offer effective skill instruction for each of 30 different skill lessons dealing with (a) seven lessons on determining main ideas, (b) eight lessons on drawing conclusions, (c) seven lessons on noting details, and (d) eight lessons on finding the sequence. The planned duration of each of the lessons was 30 min, resulting in thirty 30-min lessons.

Each skill lesson consisted of six instructional steps. The lessons were divided into the following elements: (a) anticipatory set, (b) lesson objective, (c) input and modeling, (d) guided practice and checking for understanding, (e) independent practice, and (f) assessment. A sample lesson using the explicit instruction method (Pearson, 1984) is found in the Appendix.

For the reading/skills teachers, we modeled how to offer effective skill instruction for each of 15 different skill lessons as described above; however, each lesson was taught over 2 days. The procedure resulted in four lessons on determining the main idea, four lessons on drawing conclusions, three lessons on noting details, and four lessons on finding the sequence. The planned duration of the lessons was 15 min, leaving 15 remaining min of the 30-minute treatment for free reading. The procedure resulted in thirty 15-min half lessons over the 30-day period. The reading/skills teachers were shown ways of documenting the amount of time and the titles read during the 15 min of allocated free reading time in the group.

The reading-only group teachers received instruction on teaching students how to select literature for reading and how to keep records for the time and titles students read. The entire 30-min period was devoted to the reading of student-selected books in the school media center.

Throughout the study, we monitored all the teachers by following a predetermined schedule that was not given to any of them, to ensure experimental fidelity. All the teachers were observed at least seven times during our study. Suggestions for instructional improvement were offered, if needed, following the observations. Suggestions included such elements as pacing of the lessons and the use of improved examples.

*Experimental Procedures*

The instructional procedures, as outlined, were administered by the six teachers during a regularly scheduled 30-min reading period. Either thirty 30-min lessons or thirty 15-min skill lessons, as described previously, were given over a period of 30 consecutive school days. At the conclusion of the 30-minute experimental reading period, students returned to their intact classrooms for an additional 30 min of reading and skill lessons as outlined in the Houghton Mifflin basal and the district curriculum guide. Teachers followed the basal and curriculum guide strictly during the 30-day period. The additional 30-min period of reading instruction was monitored in the same manner as the treatment groups to ensure fidelity. Thus, treatment items were held constant for all three of the experimental groups for 30 consecutive school days.

Following the completion of the treatments as outlined, the classroom teachers administered the SCST to the subjects in their original or intact classrooms, with our assistance. Students were told to answer the questions on the SCST by marking their responses in the spaces provided on the test. The children neither saw nor read any of the test items or the passages prior to the testing period. No other instructions were given in relation to the tests other than the initial directions at the beginning of the test. Two graduate research assistants who were not involved in the project used an answer key developed by the research team to score the children's responses.

**Results**

Descriptive statistics for the four comprehension skills tested in the pretest and posttest forms of the SCST are presented in Table 1. The mean posttest scores for each of the three treatment groups on each of the four comprehension skill measures were compared using analysis of covariance, with each pretest score serving as the covariate in each of the four separate ANCOVA analyses. The homogeneity of regression assumption associated with the application of ANCOVA was checked and satisfied for each of the four skill measures (noting details: $F[2, 57] = 1.66$, $p > .05$; drawing conclusions, $F[2, 57] = .48$, $p > .05$; finding the sequence, $F[2, 57] = .97$, $p > .05$; determining the main idea, $F[2, 57] = .50$, $p > .05$). All ANCOVAs were conducted within a regression model (SAS, General Linear Models) because of the unbalanced, partial replication nature of the design.

To assess the instructional effect of the treatments over the 30-day period, we entered the pre- and posttest SCST scores for all three groups into a within-groups MANCOVA analysis to check for significant pre- to posttest gains. The MANCOVA analysis revealed a significant gain from pretest to posttest on the four specific reading comprehension skills for all three groups, $F(4, 117) = 4.36$, $\lambda = 87$, $p < .0025$. The average gains from pre- to posttests across the three groups for each of the specific comprehension skill tests were: (a) noting details—25%;

**Table 1.—Fourth-Grade Means and Standard Deviations by Treatment Groups for the Four Reading Comprehension Skills Pre- and Posttests**

| Skills | Pretest | | Posttest | |
|---|---|---|---|---|
| | *M* | *SD* | *M* | *SD* |
| Drawing conclusions | | | | |
| Reading-only group | 10.2 | 3.0 | 11.2 | 2.8 |
| Skills-only group | 9.4 | 2.9 | 11.0 | 2.4 |
| Reading/skills group | 9.1 | 2.8 | 11.0 | 2.8 |
| Finding sequence | | | | |
| Reading-only group | 17.7 | 3.9 | 19.7 | 3.4 |
| Skills-only group | 17.5 | 6.2 | 18.2 | 5.6 |
| Reading/skills group | 17.9 | 3.7 | 19.2 | 3.0 |
| Main idea | | | | |
| Reading-only group | 9.8 | 2.8 | 12.2 | 2.1 |
| Skills-only group | 10.7 | 3.2 | 12.0 | 3.0 |
| Reading/skills group | 9.0 | 4.0 | 11.3 | 2.9 |
| Noting details | | | | |
| Reading-only group | 8.0 | 4.4 | 10.3 | 4.5 |
| Skills-only group | 8.1 | 3.6 | 10.0 | 3.1 |
| Reading/skills group | 8.4 | 3.4 | 10.4 | 2.8 |

(b) drawing conclusions—16%; (c) finding the sequence —8%; and (d) determining the main idea—20%. The composite mean gain from the pre- to posttests across the four specific skill tests for the three groups was 16.5%. Thus, the rival hypotheses of no growth in specific reading comprehension skills caused by the three treatments from pre- to posttest was rendered implausible.

Next, each set of pre- and posttest scores was entered into separate ANCOVA analyses to test for between-group differences on the four specific reading comprehension skills selected for this study: (a) determining main ideas, (b) drawing conclusions, (c) noting details, and (d) finding the sequence. The results of the four separate ANCOVAs, as shown in Table 2, indicated no significant differences among the three treatment groups at the conclusion of the experiment in their gains in specific reading comprehension skills. The finding is most interesting for at least two reasons. First, pre- to posttest performance of all three groups indicated significant gains in the selected reading comprehension skills. Thus, all three forms of reading instruction or practice, including sustained student-selected reading of literature books, apparently contributed equally to gains in specific reading comprehension skills as measured by the SCST. Second, the groups began the experiment with essentially equivalent pretest performance, thus ruling out threats to interpretation based on initial test performance differences.

## Discussion

The results of this study indicated a statistically significant difference between students' pretest and posttest scores on a researcher-constructed Specific Comprehension Skills Test as a result of three different reading instruction and practice conditions (reading only, reading/skills, and skills only). However, the results also showed no significant differences among the three treatment groups at the conclusion of the experiment on the posttest form of the Specific Comprehension Skills Test. One may conclude, therefore, that students made significant and essentially equivalent gains from the pretest to the posttest on four selected reading comprehension skills.

Interpretation and generalization of the findings are offered cautiously. The findings seem to indicate that time spent teaching specific reading comprehension skills contributes directly to gains on criterion-referenced tests of specific comprehension skills. The findings also seem to argue that time spent only reading or time spent in a combination of the two activities (skill instruction and practice and voluntary reading) yield essentially equivalent gains on a criterion-referenced test of four reading comprehension skills. In a limited way, our study provides evidence to support the allocation of more time spent reading in the intermediate grades without undue concern related to declining scores on criterion-referenced tests of reading comprehension skills. Although the results are not yet conclusive, they do seem to point to the possibility that time spent reading may affect criterion-referenced skill test performance in much the same way as time spent reading affects standardized reading achievement test scores (Anderson, Wilson, & Fielding, 1988).

The fact that trade-book reading produced readers who scored as well on the SCST as did students receiving instruction and practice on selected reading comprehension skills seems to require some explanation. First, in a time when the important contribution of background knowledge to comprehension is well known, as expressed in schema theory (Fielding, Wilson, & Anderson, 1986; Rumelhart, 1975; Spiro, 1980), one may reasonably expect that wide reading may elaborate a reader's background knowledge and experiences, thus leading to incremental and measurable improvements in reading comprehension.

Second, related research has shown that readers' internalization of text structures positively influences their comprehension (Mandler & Johnson, 1979; Stein & Glenn, 1982; Thorndyke, 1977; Whaley, 1981). That same research base also seems to imply that wide reading of literature and trade books can make a substantial contribution to readers' internalization of a variety of literary genre and text structures, thus leading to improvements in reading comprehension.

Third, Fielding, Wilson, and Anderson (1986) also contend that lessons devoted to discrete comprehension skills do not expose children to the richness in vocabulary nor to the variety of text structures used by authors to craft texts, thus limiting a primary source of knowledge that contributes directly to improved reading comprehension.

**Table 2.—Analysis of Covariance Summary Table for the Treatment Factor on Reading Comprehension Skills Posttests**

| | Univariate *F* tests | | | | |
|---|---|---|---|---|---|
| Measure | *df* | *SS* | *F* | *p* | $R^2$ |
| Drawing conclusions | | | | | |
| Treatment | 2 | .53 | .10 | ns | .64 |
| Within error | 57 | 149.72 | | | |
| Total | 60 | 420.98 | | | |
| Finding the sequence | | | | | |
| Treatment | 2 | 24.27 | 1.86 | ns | .64 |
| Within error | 57 | 371.31 | | | |
| Total | 60 | 1,037.93 | | | |
| Main ideas | | | | | |
| Treatment | 2 | 9.92 | 2.71 | ns | .76 |
| Within error | 57 | 104.43 | | | |
| Total | 60 | 438.36 | | | |
| Noting details | | | | | |
| Treatment | 2 | 1.63 | 0.18 | ns | .64 |
| Within error | 57 | 263.03 | | | |
| Total | 112 | 730.79 | | | |

Considering the limitations of our study, one must remain cautious about advocating the wholesale dropping of teacher-directed reading skill instruction too soon. However, the results do tend to argue for allocating equal, if not greater, amounts of time spent reading in school, particularly in the intermediate grades, without fear of declining performance on criterion-referenced tests of reading comprehension skills. Our conclusion must be tempered by the fact that this study was limited to fourth graders and to only four selected reading comprehension skills. Furthermore, the findings should neither be generalized to gains in specific decoding or study skills nor to younger, less-experienced readers. Although this study needs to be replicated and extended, it does provide limited evidence for cautiously moving toward equalizing the time spent reading books as well as practicing reading comprehension skills in the intermediate grades. Finally, our study provides limited, yet valuable decision-making information for teacher educators, administrators, and teachers related to allocating more time for reading in schools.

## APPENDIX

### Sequencing
### Lesson 1

*Anticipatory Set*

Write the following sentences on separate word strips and put them on the wall in front of the class in the order shown.

Goldilocks entered the bears' house and ate Little Bear's porridge.
The three bears found Goldilocks sleeping on Little Bear's bed and frightened her away.
Goldilocks broke Little Bear's favorite chair.
The three bears went for a walk until their porridge cooled.
Goldilocks went to sleep.

Tell them you are going to tell them a story and then read the word strips. Ask: What is wrong with the story? (out of order) Discuss why that is important. Have someone put the story in the correct order. Read it again.

Continue Anticipatory Set by relating the following story, instructing them to listen carefully, because you are going to ask some questions at the end:

During the month of November, 1981, people visited the "Street of Glass," Fifty-third Street in New York City. There they saw many glass objects of art, which appeared in stores, a bank, and the library. These visitors discovered that glass objects can be useful as well as beautiful. The glass pieces turned different colors as the lights around them turned on and off.

Now ask the following true/false questions. Ask the person giving the answer to explain why.

1. This story took place before Fifty-third Street was called the "Street of Lights." (false)
2. Before the lights around the glass pieces were turned on, the colors of the pieces did not change. (true)

*Lesson Objective*

Tell the students that during the next few weeks, they will be doing activities that will help them understand the sequence of a story.

*Input and Modeling*

Ask: What is the sequence of a story.

Remind the students that sequence means the order in which things happen. Refer back to the Goldilocks story and discuss how putting things in the correct order helps you understand what is going on.

After reading a short selection, discuss the sequence of events and demonstrate how you, the teacher, would determine the order of events in the selection.

*Guided Practice and Checking for Understanding*

Explain to the class that for the last 10 min or so of each period, you will read to them from either a book or selected pieces. After each reading period, you will take the time to discuss the sequence of events from the selection.

Read to the class from a book of your choice. This daily reading will provide continuity to the lesson and provide a chance for practicing sequencing skills.

*Independent Practice*

The children will read a selection from the Houghton Mifflin Basal Reader. After reading, they will write on a separate piece of paper the sequence of events in the story. Next, they are instructed to return to the story and check their sequence with the text.

*Assessment*

The teacher distributes two short paragraphs for the students to read. Each paragraph is followed by four sentences; the students are to number the sentences according to the sequence that these events occurred in the paragraphs. The teacher picks these up when the students are finished and checks them. Students' scores are entered in the grade records.

## REFERENCES


Anderson, R. C., Hiebert, E. H., Scott, J. A., & Wilkinson, I. A. G. (1985). *Becoming a nation of readers.* Urbana, IL: Center for the Study of Reading.

Anderson, R. C., Wilson, P. T., & Fielding, L. G. (1988). Growth in reading and how children spend their time outside of school. *Reading Research Quarterly, 23,* 285–303.

Durkin, D. (1981). Reading comprehension instruction in five basal readers. *Reading Research Quarterly, 16,* 515–544.

Durkin, D. (1984). Is there a match between what elementary teachers do and what basal reader manuals recommend? *The Reading Teacher, 37,* 734–745.

Farr, R., Tulley, M. A., & Powell, D. (1987). The evaluation and selection of basal readers. *The Elementary School Journal, 87,* 267–281.

Fielding, L. G., Wilson, P. T., & Anderson, R. C. (1986). A new focus on free reading: The role of trade books in reading instruction. In T. E. Raphael (Ed.), *The contexts of school based literacy.* New York, NY: Random House.

Fisher, C. W., Berliner, D., Filby, N., Marliave, R., Cohen, L., Dishaw, M., & Moore, J. (1978). *Teaching and learning in elementary schools: A summary of the beginning teacher evaluation study.* San Francisco, CA: Far Western Regional Laboratory for Educational Research and Development.

Goodman, K. S., Shannon, P., Freeman, Y. S., & Murphy, S. (1988). *Report card on basal readers.* New York, NY: Richard C. Owen.

Jachym, N. K., Allington, R. L., & Broikou, K. A. (1989). Estimating the cost of seat work. *The Reading Teacher, 43,* 30–37.

Leinhardt, G., Zigmond, N., & Cooley, W. (1981). Reading instruction and its effects. *American Educational Research Journal, 18,* 343-361.

Mandler, J. M., & Johnson, N. S. (1979). Remembrance of things parsed: Story structure and recall. *Cognitive Psychology, 9,* 111-151.

Mason, J. (1983). An examination of reading instruction in third and fourth grades. *The Reading Teacher, 36,* 906–913.

Morrow, L. M. (1986). Attitudes of teachers, principals, and parents toward promoting voluntary reading in the elementary school. *Reading Research and Instruction, 25,* 116–130.

Mosenthal, P. B. (1989). The whole language approach: Teachers between a rock and a hard place. *The Reading Teacher, 42,* 628–629.

Osborn, J. (1984). The purposes, uses, and contents of workbooks and some guidelines for publishers. In R. C. Anderson, J. Osborn, & R. J. Tierney (Eds.), *Learning to read in American schools: Basal readers and content texts.* Hillsdale, NJ: Lawrence Erlbaum Associates.

Osborn, J. (1985). Workbooks: Counting, matching, judging. In J. Osborn, P. T. Wilson, & R. C. Anderson (Eds.), *Reading education: Foundations for a literate America.* Lexington, MA: Lexington Books.

Pearson, P. D. (1984). Direct explicit teaching of reading comprehension. In G. G. Duffy, L. R. Roehler, & J. Mason (Eds.), *Comprehension instruction: Perspectives and suggestions* (pp. 222-233). New York, NY: Longman.

Rosenshine, B. B. (1980). Skill hierarchies in reading comprehension. In R. J. Spiro, B. C. Bruce, & W. F. Brewer (Eds.), *Theoretical issues in reading comprehension* (pp. 535-554). Hillsdale, NJ: Lawrence Erlbaum Associates.

Rumelhart, D. E. (1975). Notes on schema for stories. In D. G. Bobrow & A. M. Collins (Eds.), *Representation and understanding: Studies in cognitive science.* New York, NY: Academic Press.

Shannon, P. (1983). The use of commercial reading materials in American elementary schools. *Reading Research Quarterly, 19*, 68-85.

Shannon, P. (1989). *Broken promises: Reading instruction in twentieth century America.* Granby, MA: Bergin and Garvey.

Spiro, R. J. (1980). Constructive processes in prose comprehension and recall. in R. J. Spiro, B. C. Bruce, & W. F. Brewer (Eds.), *Theoretical issues in reading comprehension* (pp. 245-278). Hillsdale, NJ: Lawrence Erlbaum Associates.

Stein, N. L., & Glenn, C. G. (1982). An analysis of story comprehension in elementary school children. In R. Freedle (Ed.), *Discourse processing: Multidisciplinary perspective in discourse comprehension.* New York: NY: Academic Press.

Stern, P., & Shavelson, R. (1983). Reading teachers' judgments, plans, and decision making. *The Reading Teacher, 37*, 280-285.

Thorndyke, P. W. (1977). Cognitive structures in comprehension and memory of narrative discourse. *Cognitive Psychology, 9*, 77-110.

Whaley, J. F. (1981). Story grammar and reading instruction. *The Reading Teacher, 34*, 762-771.

# SELF-TEST FOR TASK 1-A

## Reading Time in School: Effect on Fourth Graders' Performance on a Criterion-Referenced Comprehension Test

**The Problem**

**The Procedures**

**The Method of Analysis**

**The Major Conclusion(s)**

# Teachers' Use of Homework in High Schools

**JOSEPH MURPHY**
**Vanderbilt University**

**KAREN DECKER**
**Parkland Community College**

ABSTRACT **In this article, we presented information on homework use from the perspective of 3,000 teachers in 92 high schools in Illinois. We provided data on the amount and frequency of homework. More important, however, we went beyond issues of time. We assessed the structure of homework in high schools. We examined the purposes for which homework is given and the types of work in which students are asked to engage. We also assessed the level of school and parental support for homework assigned by individual teachers.**

Homework is a topic that can quickly generate much discussion among educators, parents, and students. Homework has been the subject of spirited debate for over 100 years (see England & Flatley, 1985; National Education Association, 1966; and Strother, 1984, for reviews). Advocates on both sides of the issue of the importance of homework as an educational intervention have expressed their views during that time; nevertheless, Strother reports that our understanding of homework remains limited.

Most of what we know about homework relates to time, that is, how much homework is assigned by teachers and how many hours students spend completing those assignments. Historically, we know that students have been asked to do little homework. Sedlack, Wheeler, Pullin, and Cusick (1986) report, for example, that from 1930 to 1950 few students had to study more than 1 or 2 hours a week outside of school. A similar pattern was found for students in the 1970s and early 1980s at both the elementary- (Cawelti & Adkisson, 1985) and secondary-school levels (Keith, 1982; Sedlak et al., 1986; Weber, 1986). Since that time, demands for increased amounts of student homework have been an integral component of educational reform proposals (e.g., Educational Commission of the States, 1983; National Commission on Excellence in Education, 1983).

The early evidence suggests that these proposals have changed the quantity of homework assigned to American school students. For example, based on information from the 1986 National Assessment of Educational Progress test in mathematics, *Education Week* (1988) concluded that "the amount of homework has increased drastically over the last few years" (p. 23). *Education Week* reported that, in 1986, 98% of the 13-year-olds (as compared to 73% in 1982) said that homework was given daily. A comprehensive evaluation of the 1983 educational reform package in California by Guthrie and Kirst (1988) led to a similar conclusion, a substantial increase in time spent on homework between 1979–80 and 1984–85, with a leveling off thereafter. Students in Grades 6, 8, and 12 reported that they spend about 80 min per school night on their homework.

In addition to our knowledge of time allocations, we also are developing a better understanding of the effects of homework on student achievement. Important recent research findings show that structured homework assignments can have a "meaningful influence on achievement" (Keith & Page, 1985, p. 356; Guthrie & Kirst, 1988; Paschal, Weinstein, & Walberg, 1984; Walberg, Paschal, & Weinstein, 1985, 1986).[1] Findings from educational production function studies about the positive association between homework and student achievement also are being supported by conclusions from studies of teacher effects (Good & Grouws, 1977) and of effective schools (Mackenzie, 1983; Miller & Sayre, 1986; Teddlie & Stringfield, 1985; Wynne, 1980).

Beyond issues of time allocations and correlations with student achievement, however, homework is a topic that has been largely unexplored (Epstein & Pinkow, 1988; Murphy, Decker et al., 1985). We have only a surface understanding of homework as an educational intervention. We know little about how teachers provide structure and meaning to homework, for example, how they assign, mark, and incorporate homework into course grades. Most studies in this area continue to emphasize analysis only at the broadest level of examination (i.e., total amount of homework assigned). Homework is generally studied in isolation; interactive effects with other organizational variables are ignored. At the same time that we are discovering the complexity and multifaceted nature of

*Address correspondence to Joseph Murphy, Department of Educational Leadership, George Peabody College for Teachers, Vanderbilt University, Nashville, TN 37203.*

other educational variables (e.g., expectations and ability grouping), homework continues to be treated in a molar fashion and as a simplistic concept (Murphy, Decker et al., 1987). For significant exceptions to this pattern at the model level, see Epstein and Pinkow (1988), and at the empirical level see Levin (1988).[2]

In this article, we present a descriptive picture of how teachers in high schools use homework. Building on what is known about successful homework assignments (Paschal, Weinstein, & Walberg, 1984), and paralleling recent work by Epstein and Pinkow (1988) that delineates the major aspects of how homework influences teacher practices and student achievement, we attempted to fill in some of the gaps about how homework is used by high school teachers. We performed this task by presenting teacher replies to the following general questions:

1. To what extent do districts, individual schools, and subject departments have and enforce homework policies?
2. To what extent do individual teachers assign homework?
3. What are the most commonly announced purposes of assigned homework?
4. What is the most commonly used type of homework?
5. What is the frequency of assigned homework and the expected time required by students to complete homework?
6. How is homework most frequently assigned?
7. To what extent is homework checked and graded?
8. To what extent do students successfully complete assigned homework?
9. To what extent is homework computed into course grades?
10. To what extent do teachers have assistance in grading homework?
11. How long do teachers take to grade and return homework?
12. How are expectations about homework conveyed to students and parents?
13. What is the level of parental support for the completion of student homework?
14. To what extent are there formalized school structures in place to assist students in completing their homework?

## Method

### Sample

We randomly selected 100 of the approximately 700 public high schools in Illinois and invited them to participate in this study. Teachers and principals in 92 schools agreed to contribute. The schools ranged in size from 58 to 3,500 students, with a mean of 825. The schools were characterized by their principals, as follows: rural (65%), suburban (11%), central city (9%), and mediopolis (15%) (see Tables 1 and 2 for definitions). Of the 5,092 teachers in these schools, 2,986 teachers returned useable questionnaires—a 59% return rate, or average of 32 teachers from each of the 92 schools. The range was 5 to 104. (Also see Tables 1 and 2 for descriptive information about these schools.) The final sample overrepresents rural schools and underrepresents suburban schools. This finding is true because 65% of the sample schools were rural, compared to only 49% of the schools in the population. Conversely, only 11% of the sample schools were suburban, compared to 25% of the schools in the population. Also, the average rate of return from teachers in rural schools was 70% versus 53% for medium-sized city schools, 55% for suburban schools, and 52% for central city schools.

### Data Collection and Analysis

We developed a 37-item survey for this study. Questions constituted four types: forced choice, yes-no, multiple choice, and open ended. We designed our questions

**Table 1.—Number of Schools and Teachers by School Type**

| Type | Schools | Teachers | Teacher returns |
|---|---|---|---|
| Rural—town, village, or city that is not associated with an urban area and has a population of less than 2,500 or is an area with 2,500–10,000 inhabitants if it is rural in character. | 60 | 1,595 | 1,114 |
| Mediopolis—medium-sized incorporated city separate from a central city with less than 250,000 inhabitants. | 14 | 1,242 | 655 |
| Suburban—area surrounding a central city that may or may not be independently incorporated and that exists on the outskirts of a city. | 10 | 1,355 | 741 |
| Central city—the largest municipality; a metropolitan area with 2,500 or more inhabitants. | 8 | 897 | 446 |
| Totals | 92 | 5,092 | 2,986 |

Table 2.—Teachers, Schools, and Students by AFDC and Free Lunch

| | n/teachers | Schools | n/students |
|---|---|---|---|
| | *% AFDC* | | |
| No information | 717 | 13 | 11,509 |
| 0-10 | 2,764 | 57 | 39,579 |
| 11-19 | 742 | 13 | 11,146 |
| 7-20 | 869 | 9 | 14,974 |
| Total | 5,092 | 92 | 77,148 |
| | *% free lunch* | | |
| No information | 404 | 5 | 5,580 |
| 0-10 | 2,600 | 47 | 39,347 |
| 11-19 | 815 | 19 | 11,795 |
| 7-20 | 1,273 | 21 | 20,426 |
| Total | 5,092 | 92 | 77,148 |
| | *% AFDC (or % free lunch)* | | |
| No information | 135 | 3 | 1,980 |
| 0-10 | 3,078 | 61 | 45,080 |
| 11-19 | 772 | 14 | 11,534 |
| 7-20 | 1,107 | 14 | 12,554 |
| Total | 5,092 | 92 | 77,148 |

to assess activity across five components of homework: policy existence; amount/time; purpose and type; review and feedback; and parental and school support. We asked the teachers to provide information about these issues based on the first class that they taught on Wednesday mornings.

The questionnaire had gone through numerous versions. We developed and piloted the original survey in the fall of 1985. A small-scale study was then completed in 11 rural high schools in Illinois (see Murphy, Decker et al., 1987 for results). After further revisions and additions, we ran two additional pilots before the instrument used in this study was finalized.

After coding the completed surveys, we grouped together questions relating to the five aspects of homework. We used theme analysis to develop categories for the three open-ended questions. All questions were analyzed descriptively.

## Results and Discussion

### *Course Taking*

We combined information about departments in which courses were offered, tracks, and student ability levels to provide an informative picture about academic rigor in these schools (Table 3). Although 63% of the teachers in the sample were teaching academic course sections, only 26% of these sections were at the college preparatory and advanced placement levels. Consistent with other research (Murphy, Hull, & Walker, 1987; Powell, Farrar, & Cohen, 1985; Resnick & Resnick, 1985), the bulk of high school course taking in these schools occurred in the general track. This research clearly emphasized that teachers considered nearly 85% of their students to be at (55%) or above (28%) grade level. The unmistakable message in these schools was that "at grade level" students were in the general track, whereas college preparatory and advanced placement courses were used for "above grade level" students.

### *Policy*

*District, school, and department policies.* We examined the extent to which teachers' homework assignments were supported by district, school, and departmental policies. Studies on the nature of schools as formal organizations in general (Meyer & Rowan, 1975; Weick, 1976) and studies of secondary schools in particular (Herriot & Firestone, 1984), as well as studies of organizational control (Hanson, 1981) and teacher decision making (Lortie, 1975; Rosenholtz, 1985), led us to expect little formal school-level coordination on homework assignments. This hypothesis was reinforced by recent empirical work finding that teachers operate in a vacuum in this area and that decisions on homework are established by default by class participants (Cawalti & Adkisson, 1985; Murphy, Decker et al., 1987; National Center for Educational Statistics, 1985; Powell, Farrar, & Cohen, 1985).

The data from this study reinforced these findings but with one interesting twist. In general, district, school, and departmental homework policies were conspicuous by their absence. However, districts were more active in formulating homework policies (31%) than were either schools (24%) or individual departments (18%). This latter result is the opposite of what we expected to find and may be attributable, at least in part, to the recent wave of top-down reform initiative that has taken place in Illinois.

*Classroom policy.* Some of the most exciting recent work on the teaching-learning process has underscored a long-ignored reality—the importance of the individual classroom teacher as an educational policy maker (Freeman et al., 1983; Porter, 1988; Porter & Brophy, 1988). One important policy that most teachers establish is whether they assign homework. In this sample, 86% of the teachers assigned homework to the classes in question, whereas the remaining 14% did not, a finding consistent with our earlier study of rural high schools (Murphy, Decker et al., 1987).

We also investigated whether homework was assigned in an equitable fashion across tracks (Murphy, Hallinger, & Lotto, 1986; Murphy & Hallinger, in press). We found that 98% of the teachers with college preparatory or advanced placement course-sections assigned homework. In contrast, only about three quarters (77%) of the vocational classes and four fifths of the general track (83%) and special educational classes (79%) were given work to

Table 3.—Academic Classification of Courses

| Course sections (% of teachers) | | Track level (% of teachers) | | Ability level (% of students) | |
|---|---|---|---|---|---|
| Academic | | Advanced placement | 1.7 | Below grade level | 16.7 |
| English | 19 | College preparation | 24.2 | At grade level | 55.4 |
| Mathematics | 15 | General | 47.8 | Above grade level | 27.9 |
| Science | 12 | Vocational | 16.7 | Total | 100.0 |
| Social studies | 11 | Special education | 9.6 | | |
| Foreign language | 5 | Total | 100.00 | | |
| Subtotal | 63 | | | | |
| Nonacademic | | | | | |
| Business | 8 | | | | |
| Physical education | 7 | | | | |
| Health education | 4 | | | | |
| Art | 3 | | | | |
| Music | 3 | | | | |
| Industrial art | 5 | | | | |
| Drivers education | 2 | | | | |
| Agriculture | 1 | | | | |
| Subtotal | 33 | | | | |
| Other | 4 | | | | |
| Total | 100 | | | | |

be completed at home. This inequitable pattern, which has been noted elsewhere (Center for Research on Elementary and Middle Schools, 1988; Oakes, 1985; Powell, Farrar, & Cohen, 1985), places students in nonacademic streams at a disadvantage with their peers in academic tracks.

A variety of reasons were offered by the nonassigning teachers to explain the absence of homework. Theme analysis of answers to this open-ended question resulted in the development of seven categories: (1) homework done in class (41%); (2) students' need to use class equipment (22%); (3) teachers' need to supervise (11%); (4) work done in a group (8%); (5) students graded on class participation (7%); (6) limited number of textbooks (4%); and (7) other (7%). Whereas many of these explanatory categories have much surface validity, we find it difficult to justify regularly assigning homework to be completed in class. This practice defeats a major function of homework, to extend opportunity to learn by providing additional work time.

### *Amount/Time*

Two ways to increase student opportunity to learn are to enlarge the amount of time that students have to learn and to expand the amount of content they receive. The assignment of homework lends itself to both of these goals. Recent reform reports have almost uniformly called for increased homework. For example, the Forum of Educational Organizational Leaders suggested that elementary students may benefit from 1 hour of homework, whereas high school students should complete 2 or more hours of meaningful homework per night. The National Association of Secondary School Principals has recommended 20 to 30 min of homework per night per academic subject for college-bound students and about half that much time for job-bound students (SMERC Information Center, 1984). Reports from the teachers in this study provide some useful information about how much homework is being required at the high school level.

*Amount.* Teachers reported that they assigned homework on a regular basis. Nineteen percent of the group distributed homework twice a week; 22%, three times a week; 19%, four times a week; and 22%, five times a week. The average teacher assigned homework slightly less than four times per week. (See Table 4.)

*Time.* In terms of time, nearly one half (48%) of the teachers expected that the average assignment would take between 16 and 30 min to complete. Another one third (32%) recorded an average completion time between 31 and 45 min. Only 4% of the teachers assigned less than 15 or more than 60 min of homework per night. The average teacher gave approximately 30 min of homework per class period. In total, teachers assigned students about 2 hours of homework per class per week, or, assuming five classes per day with homework expectations, approximately 2 hours of homework per day—about 30 min more per day than high school students in California (Guthrie & Kirst, 1988).

### *Purpose and Type*

*Purpose.* The importance of homework assignments in promoting student learning has been established from investigations of educational productivity (Paschal, Weinstein, & Walberg, 1984), teacher effects (Good & Grouws,

1977), effective schools (Teddlie & Stringfield, 1985), and evaluation studies in the area of educational policy (Guthrie & Kirst, 1988). To be most effective, however, homework assignments must be carefully planned and tightly connected to appropriate curricular objectives (Pennsylvania State Department of Education, 1984).

We noted earlier that well-structured homework assignments promote the two goals of increasing the amount of time available for learning and extending content coverage. In addition, homework can fulfill other educational functions, such as developing independent work habits, encouraging responsibility, refining study skills, and providing opportunities for creativity (Pendergrass, 1985; Pennsylvania State Department of Education, 1985).

To examine the purposes for homework, we asked the 2,550 teachers who assigned homework to select the single most common purpose of homework assignments from a list of seven choices. In a related question, we also asked them to choose all the purposes for which they assigned homework.

Our first observation was that homework was not assigned for a wide variety of primary purposes in these schools—three answers account for 90% of the responses. As shown in Table 5, the most common purpose of homework was to reinforce class materials—to review concepts and skills introduced in class. Over one half (55%) of the sample chose this purpose as the rationale for homework assignments. Less than one quarter (23%) of the sample selected mastery of course objectives as the second most common purpose. Introduce new material was the third most common purpose, with 11% of the teachers choosing this response. Only small percentages of teachers selected preparation for a test (3%), monitor student progress (3%), or student-created independent research projects (1%) as the most common purpose.

A more highly productive picture emerged when we analyzed responses to all purposes for homework assignments. A lot of variety existed in the packages of answers selected by these teachers. Of the possible combinations available, only four were selected by more than 100 teachers. The two most common purposes, each with 17%, were (1) reinforce class material, mastery of course objectives, preparation for a test, and monitor student progress; and (2) reinforce class material, introduce new material, mastery of course objectives, preparation for a test, and monitor student progress.

*Type.* During the last 10 years, investigators have begun to examine the relationships between types of homework assignments and student academic achievement (Epstein & Pinkow, 1988; Strother, 1984). Although there are no clear answers as to which types of homework are best for students in different situations, research indicates that irrelevant or *busywork* tasks unrelated to the curriculum, identical assignments for all students, and unnecessary repetition of already learned material are examples of ineffective types of homework (Pendergrass, 1985; Lee & Pruitt, 1979).

One of our objectives was to discover which type of homework was most commonly distributed to students. Based upon earlier work by Lee and Pruitt (1979) and Pendergrass (1985), we developed seven homework types. From this list, we asked teachers to select (1) the most commonly assigned type of homework and (2) all types of homework assigned in the course (see Table 5). As with responses to *purpose*, there is not a great deal of variety in the answers to the first question. Half of the teachers chose textbook and questions as the most commonly used type of homework assignment. An additional 25% selected worksheets. The remainder of the choices were distributed throughout the types in descending order as follows: essays and writing assignments (7%); other (7%); reading and research reports (5%); independent projects (4%); and watching a television program (1%).

The responses to the second part of this question, all types of homework assigned, reinforced these findings. The combination of choices selected most by these teachers was textbook and questions and worksheets (20%); no other package of homework types accounted for more than 7% of the responses.

Two summary observations are worth noting. First, although variety in homework type is desirable (Pendergrass, 1985; Lee & Pruitt, 1979), the teachers in these high schools tended almost exclusively to distribute two kinds of assignments, textbook and questions and work-

**Table 4.—Amount and Time of Homework Assignments**

| | *Homework assigned*[a] | |
|---|---|---|
| Amount | *n* | % |
| Blank | 25 | 1.0 |
| Occasionally | 184 | 7.2 |
| Once a week | 269 | 10.5 |
| Twice a week | 473 | 18.5 |
| 3 times a week | 560 | 22.0 |
| 4 times a week | 485 | 19.0 |
| 5 times a week | 554 | 21.7 |
| Total | 2,550 | 100.0 |
| | *Time expected to complete homework assignments (in min)*[b] | |
| Time | *n* | % |
| Blank | 53 | 2.1 |
| 0–15 | 111 | 4.4 |
| 16–30 | 1,202 | 47.1 |
| 31–45 | 823 | 32.3 |
| 46–60 | 269 | 10.5 |
| 60 or more | 92 | 3.6 |
| Total | 2,550 | 100.0 |

[a]Mean, mode, median = 4; *SD* = 1.6; range = 6; Q1 = 3; Q2 = 4; Q3 = 5; Q3 − Q1 = 2.
[b]Mean 2.6; mode = 2; median = 2; *SD* = .9; range = 5; Q1 = 2; Q2 = 2; Q3 = 3; Q3 − Q1 = 1.

Table 5.—Purpose and Type of Homework Assignments

| Purpose | *n* | % |
|---|---|---|
| *Single purpose*[a] | | |
| Blank | 62 | 2.4 |
| Reinforce class material | 1,409 | 55.2 |
| Introduce new material | 275 | 10.8 |
| Mastery of course objectives | 574 | 22.5 |
| Preparation for a test | 73 | 2.9 |
| Monitor student progress | 71 | 2.8 |
| Student-created independent research project | 36 | 1.4 |
| Total | 2,551 | 100.0 |

| Type | *n* | % |
|---|---|---|
| *Single type*[b] | | |
| Blank | 47 | 1.9 |
| Worksheets | 634 | 24.9 |
| Textbook and questions | 1,263 | 49.5 |
| Essays and written assignments | 188 | 7.4 |
| Independent projects | 91 | 3.6 |
| Reading and research reports | 137 | 5.3 |
| Watching a television program | 13 | .5 |
| Other | 177 | 6.9 |
| Total | 2,550 | 100.0 |

[a]Mean = 1.4; mode = 1; median = 1; *SD* = 1.4; range = 7; Q1 = 1; Q2 = 1; Q3 = 3; Q3 − Q1 = 2.
[b]Mean 2.4; mode = 2; median = 2; *SD* = 1.7; range = 7.0; Q1 = 1; Q2 = 2; Q3 = 2; Q3 − Q1 = 1.

sheets. A corollary observation is that the types of assignments most likely to reflect higher order cognitive skills —essays and writing assignments, reading and research reports, and independent projects—were infrequently given. A better understanding of the proper balance of homework types is needed. We also need to know why teachers use only certain types of assignments. For example, are teachers distributing textbook questions and worksheets because they provide the independent practice that students need or because they lack the time required to adequately prepare and assess more complex types of homework assignments?

*Assignment, Review, Grading, and Feedback*

In their model on homework, Epstein and Pinkow (1988) outline three sets of independent variables—assignments, completion, return and follow-up—that influence both student learning and teacher practices. We have already presented much information about homework assignments in the 92 schools in our sample. In this section, we complete that discussion by examining how teachers assign homework. Next we review student homework completion rates. We then analyze how teachers review and grade homework and provide feedback to students.

*Methods of assigning homework.* One of the issues we addressed was why students often do not complete their homework.[3] Answers to many of the questions in this study provide some insight into this matter. One factor that we believed might contribute to the problem was the method teachers used when they provided assignments. We therefore checked on how and when homework assignments were made. Seventy-three percent of the teachers mostly (31%) or always (42%) assigned homework orally to the class. Forty-five percent mostly (23%) or always (22%) distributed homework along with written directions on the board. About one third mostly (17%) or always (12%) provided written directions to students. Another one third mostly (12%) or always (22%) made homework a part of the course contract. Homework was overwhelmingly assigned at the end of the class period (61%), whereas 22% of the teachers assigned it at the beginning of the period. In our further investigations, we plan to explore directly the connection between the quality of assignments and completion rates. We especially want to examine what oral assignments made at the end of a class period seem like to class participants.

*Amount of homework completed.* The majority of the teachers (51%) reported that students finished between 81% and 100% of their homework, whereas another one third (30%) declared that the completion rate was between 61% and 80%. Teachers also noted that there was a group of about one fifth of the students (19%) who completed less than 60% of their work. Whereas these numbers are better than those reported by certain students, they reveal that many homework assignments are being ignored by high school students.[3]

*Reasons for noncompletion.* Teacher reports of student excuses for failure to do homework were informative. Eleven categories were developed from teacher responses to an open-ended question on this topic. The major rationale students provided to explain their failure to complete assignments was that they forgot (40%). Other reasons given with a response rate of 6% or more were as follows: not enough time (19%), didn't understand the assignment (11%), work/job (9%), chose not to do it (7%), and too many other assignments (6%).

Two points are worth noting. First, it is not inconceivable that at least part of the problem (i.e., the forgot and didn't understand the assignment groups) could be improved by school and teacher activity, for example, better methods of assigning work, more thoroughly developed school and parental support structures. Second, time spent at work was not used as a major rationale for not completing homework. Many high school teachers are reluctant to provide homework, however, because they assume that students who have jobs will not do it. These data indicate that this assumption should be examined more fully before it becomes ingrained in the decision-making fabric of schools. The data also suggest that although time issues are important, comprising 34% of the reasons for student failure to finish homework, to a certain extent homework completion is an alterable variable that can be controlled by school staff.

*Checking homework: Amount and methods.* Most high school teachers are busy people with heavy teaching loads and concomitant paper work. Given this condition, as well as the knowledge that "the homework done must be examined by the teachers if the students are to take their assignments seriously and fulfill them conscientiously" (Adler, 1985, p. 194), we wanted to know how much of the assigned homework teachers were able to review. The answers were encouraging. Over three quarters of the teachers (76%) reported that they checked between 81% and 100% of students' work. Another 14% declared that they reviewed between 61% and 80%. Only about 1 teacher in 10 (11%) reported checking less than 60% of students' homework.

*Grading homework.* One way that teachers provide value to students' homework is to assign it a grade. We found that 88% of the teachers in these schools graded homework, whereas 12% did not. That is, almost 90% of these teachers not only checked to see that homework was finished, but also regularly provided letter or number marks on completed assignments. Nearly 70% of the teachers (69%) graded between 81% and 100% of homework, and another 14% marked between 61% and 80%. Only 17% of the teachers graded less than 60% of students' homework. Although teachers were able to mark much of the homework they distributed, opportunity costs were associated with this commitment of time. Nearly 70% of the teachers (69%) noted that the time required for grading homework sometimes (48%) or often (21%) influenced the amount or type of assignments that they made. Further analysis of this cost is needed, along with an analysis of the costs of grading homework on other aspects of the teaching process, such as planning lessons (Epstein & Pinkow, 1988).

In general, these teachers did not have much assistance in grading student work. Almost three quarters of the group (70%) graded nearly all student homework themselves. Of those who did have help, most of it was provided by teacher aides (63%). Few instructors relied on student aides (16%) or students grading work during class time (14%) to reduce the amount of grading that they needed to do.

*Feedback to students.* Two aspects of this issue lent themselves to analysis by questionnaire—how much time teachers take to grade and return homework and how important homework marks are in determining course grades. Teachers reported that they were diligent in returning student homework assignments. Three quarters of the group graded and returned assignments in 1 (43%) or 2 (32%) days; only 10% took more than 4 days. Not surprisingly, 97% of those who graded homework computed these marks into students' semester grades. Much diversity existed, however, in the amount of importance teachers attached to homework grades. Although the average (mode) teacher (18%) counted homework as 20% of the semester grade, 13% used it for less than 10% of the grade, whereas 18% of the teachers counted it as 40% or more.

A picture of how much significance teachers attributed to homework marks in developing semester grades can be seen by examining key divisions within the data: 5% of grade (2% of teachers), 10% of grade (11% of teachers), 15% of grade (6% of teachers), 20% of grade (18% of teachers), 25% of grade (15% of teachers), 30% of grade (8% of teachers), 35% of grade (6% of teachers), 40% of grade (7% of teachers), 45% of grade (1% of teachers), 50% of grade or higher (11% of teachers).

*Success rate.* Recent research has firmly established the connection between high rates of success and student learning (Brophy & Good, 1986). The picture developed by these teachers on the topic of success leaves room for improvement. Remembering that nearly 80% of the assigned homework consisted of independent practice type activities (see Table 5), one would expect success rates of 90% or higher. Yet, according to their teachers, only 6% of the students reached that level of accuracy. An additional 33% of the students experienced success rates of between 81% and 90%, and 38% more were between 71% and 80%. Nearly one quarter of the students (23%) were successful less than 70% of the time.

### *School and Parental Support*

One of the suppositions with which we began our study was that homework would be taken more seriously by students when there were school-wide structures that supported the efforts of individual teachers. We developed this hypothesis primarily from studies of effective schools that show that these organizations tend to operate as organic units, with much consistency and coordination among staff, rather than as collections of individual teachers (Mortimer & Sammons, 1988; Rutter, Maughan, Mortimore, & Ouston, 1979). A second supposition was that students would attribute greater importance to homework when it was supported by their parents. This hypothesis was again drawn from studies of effective schools (Brookover et al., 1982; Cotton & Savard, 1980; Teddlie & Stringfield, 1985) and has been dramatically reinforced by the recent work of Chubb (1988) who concluded that "the largest estimated influence on the effectiveness of school organization is the role of parents in the school" (p. 56).

Our analysis revealed that school and environmental (parental) sources were not heavily employed to reinforce the importance of homework in these schools. At the school level, we have noted the absence of supportive homework policies. In addition, 62% of the teachers reported that there were no formal school structures to assist students in completing homework assignments.

In terms of securing parental involvement and support, only 57% of the instructors communicated their expectations about homework to parents. This finding is consistent with those from a recent study in South Carolina (South Carolina State Board of Education, 1987) that found that only one third of the parents knew the homework rules for their children's schools. Clearly, it is difficult for parents to be involved in activities of which they have no knowledge.

An examination of the responses from the approximately 1,400 teachers who did communicate homework expectations to parents revealed that the teachers did so primarily through regular school mechanisms: class letters (24%), open houses (20%), progress reports (20%), telephone calls (19%), parent conferences (14%), other answers (3%). Teachers' assessments of parental support for completion of homework—poor (20%), satisfactory (34%), good (35%), and excellent (11%)—may be subject to improvement through stronger efforts to communicate homework expectations to parents and to involve them directly in this facet of their children's school work.

**Conclusion**

In this article we presented information on homework from the perspective of 3,000 teachers in 92 high schools in Illinois. We provided additional data on the amount of homework teachers assign. Our findings in this area are consistent with other recent reports that show that students are completing considerably more homework than they did 10 years ago. More important, however, we went beyond issues of time. We pushed deeply into the structure of homework in high schools. We examined the purposes for which homework is given and the types of work in which students are asked to engage. We investigated how teachers assign, review, and grade student work. We examined the level of school and parental support for homework assigned by individual teachers. We also looked at student responses to homework through the eyes of their teachers.

We relied upon a questionnaire to tap into the perceptions of teachers. Other methods of investigation, document analysis, in-depth interviewing, classroom observation, along with sources of information, student work products, and parent perceptions, are available to supplement and expand our findings. Irrespective of which investigative tools are selected, however, the path for future studies in the area of homework is becoming more clearly delineated. Future studies will need better theoretical and conceptual grounding. Researchers will need to deal more accurately with the complexities of homework as an educational intervention.

In particular, variables that mediate between homework's impact on student learning and teacher behavior must be more carefully specified. The operation of these bridging factors in varying contexts must be examined. The number of dependent variables in homework studies should be increased. Student outcomes other than achievement should be employed. The loop between homework and teacher practices needs much exploration. Finally, some attention will need to be devoted to the opportunity costs associated with homework, both for students and for teachers.

**ACKNOWLEDGMENTS**

This research was supported by grants from the University of Illinois and the Jane A. Hale Foundation. We acknowledge this support. We also acknowledge the assistance of Michael Connell in helping us compile the data for this analysis.

**NOTES**

1. This conclusion has been challenged elsewhere. See, for example, Levine, 1988.
2. Epstein and Pinkow (Center for Research on Elementary and Secondary Schools, 1988) have found, for example, that "the relationship between homework time and achievement seems to differ at the elementary, middle, and high school levels" (p. 1). Levine (1988) has concluded that the connection between amount of homework and reading achievement is heavily mediated by type of community and parental education.
3. For example, in a comprehensive analysis of this issue in South Carolina (South Carolina State Board of Education, 1987), researchers discovered that only one half of the students reported that their peers handed in homework on time.

**REFERENCES**

Adler, M. J. (1985). The Paideia proposal. In B. Gross & R. Gross (Eds.), *The great school debate.* New York: Simon & Schuster.

Brookover, W., Beamer, L., Efthim, H., Hathaway, D., Lezotte, L., Miller, S., Passalacqua, J., & Tornatzky, L. (1982). *Creating effective schools: An in-service program for enhancing school learning climate and achievement.* Holmes Beach, FL: Learning Publications.

Brophy, J., & Good, T. L. (1986). Teacher behavior and student achievement. In M. Wittrock (Ed.), *The handbook of research on teaching* (3rd ed.) New York: Macmillan.

Cawelti, A., & Adkisson, J. (1985, April). ASCD study reveals elementary school time allocations for subject areas: Other trends noted. *ASCD Curriculum Update,* 1-11.

Center for Research on Elementary and Middle Schools (1988, June). Newsletter.

Chubb, J. E. (1988, Winter). Why the current wave of school reform will fail. *The Public Interest.* (90), 28-49.

Cotton, K., & Savard, W. G. (1980, December). *Parent participation.* Paper prepared for Alaska Department of Education, Office of Planning and Research. Audit and Evaluation Program, Northwest Regional Educational Laboratory, Portland, OR.

Educational Commission of the States (1983). *Action for excellence.* Denver: Author.

*Education Week* (1988, June). 7(38), 23.

England, D. A., & Flatley, J. K. (1985). *Homework—and why.* Bloomington, IN: Phi Delta Kappa.

Epstein, J. L., & Pinkow, L. (1988, April). *Homework: U.S. and international studies, issues, and models.* Paper presented at the annual meeting of the American Educational Research Association, New Orleans.

Freeman, D. J., Kuhs, T. M., Porter, A. C., Floden, R. E., Schmidt, W. H., & Schwille, J. R. (1983, May.) Do textbooks and tests define a national curriculum in elementary school mathematics? *Elementary School Journal, 83*(5), 501-503.

Good, T. L., & Grouws, D. (1977, May/June). Teacher effects: A process-product study in fourth grade mathematics classrooms. *Journal of Teacher Education, 28,* 49-54.

Guthrie, J. W., & Kirst, M. W. (1988, March). *Conditions of education in California 1988.* Berkeley: Policy Analysis for California Education. (Policy Paper No. 88-3-2).

Hanson, E. M. (1981). Organizational control in educational systems: A case study of governance in schools. In S. B. Bacharach (Ed.),

*Organizational behavior in schools and school districts.* New York: Praeger.

Herriott, R. E., & Firestone, W. A. (1984, Fall). Two images of schools as organizations: A refinement and elaboration. *Educational Administration Quarterly, 20*(4), 41-57.

Keith, T. (1982, April). Time spent on homework and high school grades: A large sample path analysis. *Journal of Educational Psychology, 74*(2), 248-253.

Keith, T., & Page, E. (1985). Homework works at school: National evidence for policy changes. *School Psychology Review, 14*(3), 351-359.

Lee, J. F., & Pruitt, K. W. (1979, September). Homework assignments: Classroom games or teaching tools. *The Clearing House, 53*(1), 31-35.

Levine, D. V. (1988, April). *Homework and reading achievement in NAEP data on thirteen-year-olds.* Paper presented at the annual meeting of the American Educational Research Association, New Orleans.

Lortie, D. C. (1975). *The schoolteacher: A sociological study.* Chicago: The University of Chicago Press.

Mackenzie, D. E. (1983, April). Research for school improvement: An appraisal of some recent trends. *Educational Researcher, 12*(4), 6-16.

Meyer, J. W., & Rowan, B. (1975, August). *Notes on the structure of educational organizations: Revised version.* Paper presented at the annual meeting of the American Sociological Association, San Francisco.

Miller, S. K., & Sayre, K. A. (1986, April). *Case studies of affluent effective schools.* Paper presented at the annual meeting of the American Educational Research Association, San Francisco.

Mortimore, P., & Sammons, P. (1988, September). New evidence on effective elementary schools. *Educational Leadership, 45*(1), 4-8.

Murphy, J., Decker, K., Chaplin, C., Dagenais, R., Heller, J., Jones, R., & Willis, M. (1987, Spring). An exploratory analysis of the structure of homework assignments in high school. *Research in Rural Education, 4*(2), 61-71.

Murphy, J., & Hallinger, P. (in press). Equity as access to learning: Curricular and instructional treatment differentials. *Journal of Curriculum Studies.*

Murphy, J., Hallinger, P., & Lotto, L. S. (1986, November/December). Inequitable allocations of alterable learning variables in schools and classrooms. *Journal of Teacher Education, 37*(6), 21-26.

Murphy, J., Hull, T., & Walker, A. (1987, July/August). Academic drift and curricular debris: An analysis of high school course-taking patterns with implications for local policy makers. *Journal of Curriculum Studies, 19*(4), 341-360.

National Center for Educational Statistics (1985, June). *Academic requirements and achievements in high schools.* FRSS Report No. 15. Author.

National Commission on Excellence in Education (1983, April). *A nation at risk: The imperative of educational reform.* Washington, DC: U.S. Government Printing Office.

National Education Association (1966). *Homework.* Research Summary 1966-S2. Washington, DC: Author.

Oakes, J. (1985). *Keeping track: How schools structure inequality.* New Haven, CT: Yale University Press.

Paschal, R. A., Weinstein, T., & Walberg, H. J. (1984, November/December). The effects of homework on learning: A quantitative synthesis. *The Journal of Educational Research, 78*(2), 97-104.

Pendergrass, R. A. (1985, March). Homework: Is it really a basic? *The Clearing House, 58*(7), 310-314.

Pennsylvania State Department of Education (1984). *Homework policies and guidelines.* Harrisburg, PA: Pennsylvania State Department of Education. (ERIC Document Reproduction Service No. ED 254 902).

Porter, A. C. (1988, April). *External standards and good teaching: The pros and cons of telling teachers what to do.* Paper presented at the annual meeting of the American Educational Research Association, New Orleans.

Porter, A. C., & Brophy, J. (1988, May). Synthesis of research on good teaching. Insights from the work of the Institute for Research on Teaching. *Educational Leadership, 45*(8), 74-85.

Powell, A. G., Farrar, E., & Cohen, D. K. (1985). *The shopping mall high school: Winners and losers in the educational marketplace.* Boston: Houghton Mifflin.

Resnick, D. P., & Resnick, L. B. (1985, April). Standards, curriculum, and performance: A historical and comparative perspective. *Educational Researcher, 14*(4), 5-20.

Rosenholtz, S. J. (1985, May). Effective schools: Interpreting the evidence. *American Journal of Education, 93*(2), 352-389.

Rutter, M., Maughan, B., Mortimore, P., & Ouston, J. (1979). *Fifteen thousand hours: Secondary schools and their effects on children.* Cambridge, MA: Harvard University Press.

Sedlak, M. W., Wheeler, C. W., Pullin, D. C., & Cusick, P. A. (1986). *Selling students short: Classroom bargains and academic reform in the American high school.* New York: Teachers College Press.

SMERC Information Center (1984). *The educator's digest of reform.* Redwood City, CA: San Mateo County Office of Education.

South Carolina State Board of Education (1987). *What is the penny buying for South Carolina?* Columbia, SC: Author.

Strother, D. B. (1984, February). Homework: Too much, just right, or not enough? *Phi Delta Kappan, 65*(6), 423-426.

Teddlie, C., & Stringfield, S. (1985, April). *Six different kinds of effective and ineffective schools.* Paper presented at the annual meeting of the American Educational Research Association, Chicago.

Walberg, H. J., Paschal, R. A., & Weinstein, T. (1985, April). Homework's powerful effects on learning. *Educational Leadership, 42*(7), 76-79.

Walberg, H. J., Paschal, R. A., & Weinstein, T. (1986, May). Effective schools use homework effectively. *Educational Leadership, 43*(8), 58.

Weber, J. C. (1986, April/March). School reform is rolling—But are students rolling along? *Illinois School Board Journal, 54*(2), 7-9.

Weick, K. E. (1976, March). Educational organizations as coupled systems. *Administrative Science Quarterly, 21*(1), 1-19.

Wynne, E. (1980). *Looking at schools: Good, bad, and indifferent.* Lexington, MA: D. C. Heath.

# SELF-TEST FOR TASK 1-A

## Teachers' Use of Homework in High Schools

**The Problem**

**The Procedures**

**The Method of Analysis**

**The Major Conclusion(s)**

# The Accuracy of Principals' Judgments of Teacher Performance

DONALD M. MEDLEY
University of Virginia

HOMER COKER
Georgia State University

ABSTRACT **This is a study of the accuracy of principals' judgments of teacher performance as predictors of teacher effectiveness. For each of 46 elementary school principals, correlations were obtained between judgments of effectiveness of teachers in three roles and gains of students in their classes in arithmetic and reading. The mean accuracy of judgments of teacher effectiveness in helping students acquire fundamental knowledge was .20, and there were no significant differences in the accuracy of judgments made by different principals. There was evidence the judgments of teachers of grades 3 and 5 were more accurate than judgments of teachers of grades 2, 4, and 6. Possible explanations of the low accuracy of the judgments are discussed.**

Just about every important decision about teacher utilization—whether the teacher is certified as competent, hired, receives tenure, is recognized as meritorious—depends on someone's judgment of how well that teacher performs in the classroom. The future of public education depends very much on whether these are correct in the sense that more effective teachers are more likely to be certified, hired, tenured, and recognized than less effective ones, that is, on the accuracy of the judgments of teacher performance on which they are based. Evidence about the accuracy of such judgments as predictors of teacher effectiveness is hard to come by. Their accuracy may be said to be assumed rather than proven.

Often the judgments are informal. When they are formal, they are usually recorded as ratings on a multifactor teacher rating scale. Multifactor teacher rating scales seem to have first caught educators' attention in 1915 when the yearbook of the National Society for the Study of Education was devoted to a study of such an instrument (Boyce, 1915). A multifactor teacher rating scale confronts the judge with a list of teacher characteristics believed to be related to teacher effectiveness; the judge indicates his or her opinion of the status of the teacher on each characteristic being evaluated by recording a number. The numbers assigned to all of the characteristics are then combined in some way to yield an overall evaluation of the teacher's performance.

The use of this device spread rapidly. It was easy to develop, easy and inexpensive to use, and it had high face validity. By 1930 several hundred different teacher rating scales were being used throughout the country (Barr, 1930). The powerful effect that the rater's overall impression of the person being rated has on ratings on individual characteristics had been recognized for some time (Wells, 1907) and became known as the "halo effect" (Rugg, 1922).

The halo effect, by insuring that the teacher who looked most effective to the rater was the one who got the highest rating, had a lot to do with the high face validity of the rating scale. What appears to have been the first empirical test of the accuracy of teacher ratings was published just a few years after Boyce's study (Hill, 1921). Although this pioneer study reported one correlation with teacher effectiveness, measured in terms of students' gains in achievement tests of .45, the median correlation was only .24. Since the halo effect virtually determines the ratings teachers get, the actual validity of the ratings would seem to depend almost entirely on the accuracy of the rater's judgments of teacher performance; as a result, these findings cast doubt, not just on the validity of teacher ratings, but on the accuracy of principals' judgments of teacher performance as well.

These doubts were augmented during the next 25 years, during which at least 11 additional studies of this problem were published, all of which reached the same conclusion: that the correlations between the average principal's ratings of teacher performance and direct measures of teacher effectiveness were near zero (Anderson, 1954; Barr, Torgerson, Johnson, Lyon, & Walvoord, 1935; Brookover, 1945; Gotham, 1945; Hell-

*We gratefully acknowledge support for this study under grant No. NIE-G-82-0029 from the National Institute of Education. The conclusions reported and opinions expressed are those of the authors and do not necessarily reflect the views of the Institute.* *Address correspondence to Donald M. Medley, Department of Educational Research and Evaluation, University of Virginia, Charlottesville, VA 22903.*

fritsch, 1945; Hill, 1921; Jayne, 1945; Jones, 1946; LaDuke, 1945; Lins, 1946; Medley and Mitzel, 1959). The doubts raised in these studies had no visible effect on the practice of teacher evaluation. To this day, almost all educational personnel decisions are based on judgments which, according to the research, are only slightly more accurate than they would be if they were based on pure chance.

**Statement of the Problem**

A review of these earlier studies suggests that certain limitations in the methodology and instrumentation available when they were done might account for the negative results reported. Among these limitations are the following:

1. Contamination by inter-school differences. In order to obtain a sample of teachers large enough to yield stable correlation estimates, each investigator found it necessary to draw a sample of teachers from more than one school. This made it necessary to intermingle ratings made by different principals in estimating a correlation. Differences among principals in observational skill, concepts of effective teaching, and ability to judge teacher performance could distort and therefore attenuate the correlation estimates obtained and mask any relationship that may exist.

2. Content relevance of tests. For similar reasons each investigator used the same achievement test in all of the schools in the sample studied. Differences in objectives of different schools resulted in differences in the fit between the objectives measured by the test and objectives sought by different teachers, and further distorted (and therefore underestimated) the correlations.

3. Violated assumptions. Statistical techniques used to isolate the teacher's contribution to student learning from that of other factors (especially student ability and previous achievement) involved assumptions not likely to be fulfilled, including the assumption that the correlation of student ability and previous achievement with end-of-year achievement is equal in different teachers' classes.

4. Regression artifact. Statistical procedures used to measure teacher effectiveness from student test scores were based on the achievement gain of the average student in each teacher's class. Since classes differ widely in average ability, it was necessary to base comparisons between teachers on gains of students of different ability, and then make statistical adjustments to compensate. It has been shown that, because of an artifact of regression, these adjustments tend to exaggerate the differences instead of reducing them (Campbell & Erlebacher, 1971).

By taking advantage of advances in instrumentation and in statistical methodology it was possible to design the present study, which is free from all four of these limitations. In addition, this study is focused directly on the accuracy of principals' judgments of teacher performance, instead of on the validity of principals' ratings. The study addresses three specific questions:

1. How accurate, on the average, are principals' judgments of the performance of the teachers they supervise?

2. Does the accuracy of principals' judgments of the performance of the teachers they supervise depend on which principal makes the judgements? If some principals are good judges of teacher performance and some are not, it is important to know which is which.

3. Is there any relationship between the accuracy of a principal's judgment of the performance of a teacher and (a) the grade level the teacher teaches, (b) the ability of the student whose achievement gain is measured, or (c) the achievement gains as measured in reading or mathematics? The importance of this question depends on the answers to the first two questions. If validities of principals' judgments vary, it becomes important to understand what factors are related to these variations.

**Procedures**

*Instrumentation*

The main variables measured in this study were principals' judgments of teacher performance and direct measures of teachers' effects on students based on achievement test scores. *Principals' judgments* were recorded on the form shown in the Appendix. This form was originally developed and used in an earlier study. (Medley & Mitzel, 1959). The reliability coefficient reported in the earlier study was .89, estimated from interjudge agreement. This form was chosen, first, because instead of ratings of specific teacher characteristics it yielded reliable overall judgments of teacher performance, and, second, because it was easy for the principal to use. *Teacher effectiveness* in teaching reading and arithmetic was estimated from students' pretest scores obtained at the beginning of the school year, and posttest scores obtained at the end of the same school year, on two standardized achievement tests, one of reading and one of arithmetic.

*Design Features*

The following steps were taken to avoid the limitations in earlier studies described above:

*Contamination by inter-school differences.* All correlations were estimated from variation and covariation within the same school, so that judgments made by different principals were not intermixed and could not distort the correlation estimates.

*Content relevance of tests.* The tests used in each class in this study were those administered as part of the regular testing program of the school in which the class was located. This insured that the effectivensss of each teacher was measured in terms of success in achieving goals defined by the school, not by the researcher. It also meant that test scores of students in different schools were not comparable (except when both schools happened to use the same test). But because all correlations were estimated from variation and covariation within the same school, no comparisons were made between test scores of students in different schools, and there was no need for such comparability.

*Violated assumptions.* Teacher effectiveness was estimated in this study by a statistical procedure radically different from those used in the earlier studies. Posttest scores on each test were regressed on pretest scores on the same test separately within each class. Thus a regression equation was obtained for predicting posttest scores from pretest scores in that teacher's class only. The predicted posttest score of a student with any given pretest score obtained in this way will be referred to as the estimated gain score (EGS) for that kind of student in that teacher's class.

In an earlier study it was found that different teachers are most effective with students at different ability levels (Lara, 1983). Therefore, each teacher's regression equation was used to estimate two EGS's for each teacher: one was the EGS of a student of high ability, that is, one whose pretest score was at the 86th percentile of the local norms on that test; the other was the EGS of a student of low ability, that is, one whose pretest score was at the 16th percentile of the local norms on the test. EGS's were estimated for reading and for arithmetic, yielding in all four measures of the effectiveness of each teacher.

Because all EGS's were based on students with the same pretest score, the same ability, they may be interpreted as measures of relative gains in different teachers' classes. For this reason, and because they are estimated entirely from data within the teacher's own class, the assumptions required by the procedures used in the earlier studies are not needed. In particular, instead of assuming that correlations within different classes are equal, this procedure uses the differences between them to improve the estimate of teacher effectiveness.

*Regression artifact.* Since a teacher's EGS score is estimated from within-class variation and covariation only, the artifact of regression does not distort the correlations as it does when older methods are used (Baldwin, Medley, & MacDougall, 1984).

The EGS score as defined is probably best described as a de facto estimate of teacher effectiveness, since it does not isolate the part of the student's achievement gain attributable to the teacher's efforts from the part due to characteristics of the teacher's class that might affect student learning. If desired, these other factors could be eliminated by using the technique of partial correlation to estimate the correlation between EGS's and other variables, such as principals' judgments. This might be important in a basic research study, but what matters in a practical situation is the de facto effectiveness of the teacher, and this is what a principal should be best able to judge.

### Data Collection

The sample of teachers used in the study was obtained by first drawing a sample of principals and then using only those teachers whose performance they were willing to judge. School sytems in the souteastern United States whose testing programs provided scores on equivalent forms of a reading test and an arithmetic test obtained at the beginning and ending of the same school year were approached. Permission was sought to ask principals in each system to participate in the study. Forty-six principals agreed to participate. The final sample of teachers consisted of 87 groups of elementary-school teachers, each made up of teachers of the same grade and subject in the same school whose performance had been judged by the same principal. The total number of teachers for whom complete data were available was 322.

### Data Analysis

Coefficients of correlation were calculated separately in each of the 87 groups between the four EGS's of each teacher and the principal's judgment of the teacher's performance of each of the three roles. In order to provide an internal estimate of error, each of the 322 classes was split into two random halves and each correlation coefficient was estimated twice, once on each half of the class. Because the number of classes per grade in any one school was small, the number of teachers in each of the 87 groups was also small, and the individual correlation estimates obtained were quite unstable. However, the number of correlations was large enough so that the various estimates of mean correlations calculated in the data analysis were stable enough to provide answers to the principal questions of the study.

The number of correlations calculated for each principal was 24G, where $G$ represents the number of grade groups judged by the principal. The set of correlations for each of the 46 principals was submitted to an analysis of variance in which the dependent variable was a correlation coefficient. The independent variables were: Student Ability (A), Subject Tested (S), Role Judged (R), and, for those principals who recorded judgments of teachers in two or more grades, Grade Taught (G). The design was conceptualized as a four-way factorial, $2 \times 2 \times 3 \times G$, with the difference between correlations based on different halves of the same class providing the estimate of error with 12G degrees of freedom. Components of variance associated with each source of variation were estimated in each of the 46 analyses, and then averaged across all principals to provide estimates of the relative importance of each factor in determining the validity of the average principal's judgments.

This analysis revealed, among other things, that principals' judgments of teachers' performance of different roles were interchangeable. This made it possible to answer the second of the three questions by doing a repeated measures analysis of variance of the mean correlation for each group and role. The dependent variables in this analysis were Roles, Principals, and Groups of Teachers within Principals.

### Results

Before the findings directly relevant to each of the three major questions are presented, one unanticipated finding should be noted. These principals regarded their teachers as far superior to teachers in other schools. When they were asked to estimate the performance of the 322 teachers in the sample they reported that 87% of them were above average in performing Role 1; that the average teacher in the sample outperformed 85% of other teachers of the same grade and subject; and that more than 13% of these teachers outperformed all other teachers of their grade and subject.

The first question relating to the accuracy, on the average, of principals' judgments of the performance of the teachers they supervise is answered in Table 1. A mean correlation of .17 over all roles, and a mean correlation with a principal's judgment of a teacher's performance of Role 1 (the most relevant one) of .20 are shown.

Whether the accuracy of principals' judgments of the performance of the teachers they supervise depend on which principal makes the judgments is answered in Table 2. If the principals differ in their ability to make accurate judgments of the teachers they supervise, then the mean square between principals in this analysis should be significantly larger than the mean square within principals. The relevant value of Snedecor's $F$ is only 1.19, indicating no significant difference.

The third question as to the relationship between the accuracy of a principal's judgment and (a) the grade level the teacher teaches, (b) the ability of the student whose achievement gain is measured, or (c) the achievement gains are measured in reading or mathematics is answered in Table 3.

It is clear from Table 3 that neither the role judged, the subject tested, nor the ability of the student bears much relationship to the accuracy of these principals' judgments, but that the grade taught does. The main effect for Grade Taught alone accounted for 17.7% of the variance in accuracy of the judgments, and interactions between Grade Taught and other factors accounted for another 31.6% for a total of 49.3%. This is almost three fourths of the explained variance, and is substantially greater than the residual or unexplained variance.

It is interesting to note that judgments of teachers of grades 3 and 5 (odd numbered grades) appear to be more accurate than judgments of teachers of grades 2, 4, or 6 (even numbered grades).

**Table 1.—Mean Correlations Between Principals' Judgments of Teacher Performance in Three Roles and Expected Gains of Pupils in the Teachers' Classes**

| Grade | *n* | Role 1 | Role 2 | Role 3 | Average |
|---|---|---|---|---|---|
| 2 | 30 | 0.20 | 0.13 | 0.02 | 0.12 |
| 3 | 10 | 0.26 | 0.24 | 0.22 | 0.24 |
| 4 | 12 | 0.16 | 0.10 | 0.05 | 0.10 |
| 5 | 16 | 0.23 | 0.22 | 0.25 | 0.23 |
| 6 | 19 | 0.17 | 0.24 | 0.13 | 0.18 |
| Overall | 87 | 0.20 | 0.19 | 0.13 | 0.17 |

**Table 2.—Analysis of Variance of Correlations Between Principals' Judgments of Performance of 87 Groups of Teachers in Three Roles and Expected Achievement Gains of Students in the Teachers' Classes**

| Source of variation | *df* | Sum of squares | *M*² | *F*-Ratio |
|---|---|---|---|---|
| Role rated | 2 | 0.3488 | 0.174 | 0.48 |
| Principal | 45 | 19.4288 | 0.432 | 1.19 |
| Group (same principal) | 41 | 14.9144 | 0.364 | 10.05 |
| Interaction (R × P) | 90 | 4.5356 | 0.050 | 1.39 |
| Residual variation | 82 | 2.9670 | 0.036 | |
| Total variation | 260 | 42.1946 | | |

### Discussion

The most important finding of this study is the low accuracy of the average principal's judgments of the performance of the teachers he or she supervises. What is particularly striking about this finding is its consistency with the findings of the earlier studies, and the clear implication that the negative findings of the earlier studies cannot be blamed on any limitations in instrumentation or methodology. Failure to reject the null hypothesis does not, of course, prove that it is true; when so many different studies yield estimated correlations so nearly equal, the conclusion that the true correlation is near .20 becomes quite plausible. In any case, this research provides no support whatever for the widely held belief that the average principal is a good judge of teacher performance.

Why should this be? For one thing, it is far more difficult to judge teacher performance than is generally realized. The procedure used to obtain the measurements of teacher effectiveness the principals' judgments are supposed to predict requires (a) obtaining estimates of the test scores of every student in the class at the beginning and at the end of a school term, (b) estimating two regression coefficients from these scores, (c) deriving an estimate of the posttest score corresponding to an arbitrarily chosen pretest score from these coefficients, and (c) comparing this posttest score with posttest scores of other teachers estimated in the same way.

Since such a procedure could not be used or even approximated by any principal, a principal's judgment must be based on observations, formal and informal, of teachers' and students' behaviors while the teaching and learning is going on, and on comparisons between those behaviors and the principal's own conception or model of effective teacher behavior. Reasonable as this procedure seems, the research clearly indicates that it is not working. Why not? Is it because principals are not very good observers, because their conceptions or models of effective teacher behavior are erroneous, or because although they possess these abilities for some reason they cannot or do not use them?

Any or all of these questions could be answered affirmatively. Experience gained in the process-product research indicates that it is far more difficult to make objective and accurate observations of the behavior of teachers and students than is generally realized (Medley, Coker, & Soar, 1984, pp. 99-109). Most students of teacher effectiveness agree that there are sizable gaps in present knowledge of the nature of effective teacher behavior, gaps which make it impossible to provide conceptions or models complete enough to serve as adequate basis for teacher evaluation.

**Table 3.—Percentages of Variance in Correlations Between Principals' Judgments of Teacher Performance and Expected Gains of the Teachers' Students Associated With Selected Contextual Factors**

| Factor | Percentage of variance |
|---|---|
| Teacher role rated | 1.6 |
| Subject tested | 4.1 |
| Grade taught | 17.7 |
| Pupil ability | 4.5 |
| Interaction R × S | 0.1 |
| Interaction R × G | 3.5 |
| Interaction R × A | 0.3 |
| Interaction S × G | 7.8 |
| Interaction S × A | 7.1 |
| Interaction G × A | 10.3 |
| Interaction R × S × G | 0.5 |
| Interaction R × S × A | 0.0 |
| Interaction R × G × A | 0.4 |
| Interaction S × G × A | 8.2 |
| Interaction R × S × G × A | 0.0 |
| Residual variation | 33.0 |
| Total | 100.0 |

*Note.* The above table is based on ratings by 24 principals.

The second major outcome of this study was the failure to find evidence that principals vary in their ability to judge teacher performance. The explanation of this may lie in the low stability of the individual estimates of correlations obtained in the study; there is a possibility that such variations do exist but were not detected. Unless this finding is verified it should therefore be disregarded. This is a good thing, because acceptance of both of these findings would imply that all principals are unable to judge teacher performance accurately.

The finding that the accuracy of judgments of teacher performance is related to the grade level taught by the teacher whose performance is being judged is perhaps of more theoretical than practical interest, since the highest correlation in any grade was .26—too small to be useful.

Efforts to improve the quality of teachers, whether by better recruitment and selection, upgraded inservice training, or more efficient teacher utilization all depend on the ability to detect differences in teacher performance on demand, promptly, economically, and accurately. Can principals be trained to be better observers of classroom behavior? Can they develop more accurate conceptions or models of effective teaching? Can they be persuaded to devote the amount of their time and effort to teacher evaluation necessary to put this knowledge to use? Or should the use of principals' judgments be abandoned and some better way of assessing teacher performance be developed?

## APPENDIX

Instructions to Principals

Teachers in today's schools must perform competently in at least three roles in order to be successful. You are being asked to share with us your best judgment as to how well the teacher named above fulfills each of them in your school as a teacher of the subject named.

Please indicate your judgment by writing a number between one and twenty in the space before the description of each role printed below. The number should indicate where you think the teacher would rank in a representative group of teachers in that subject and grade. If the teacher performs better than all the rest, write 20; if all the others perform better than this teacher, write 1; and so on.

All ratings will be kept confidential; no one except the clerk who transcribes the data (and removes all names) will know the name of either the teacher or the principal involved. These sheets will be destroyed as soon as the data have been transcribed.

____ Role I — The teacher is responsible for providing learning experiences which result in pupils' acquisition of fundamental knowledge.

____ Role II — The teacher is responsible for providing children with learning experiences which lead to good citizenship, personal satisfaction, and self understanding.

____ Role III — The teacher is a professional colleague of other teachers, supervisors, and administrators.

## REFERENCES

Anderson, H. M. (1954). A study of certain criteria of teaching effectiveness. *Journal of Experimental Education*, *23*, 41-71.

Baldwin, L., Medley, D. M., & MacDougall, M. A. (1984). A comparison of analysis of covariance to within-class regression in the analysis of non-equivalent groups. *Journal of Experimental Education, 52*, 68-76.

Barr, A. S. (1930). What qualities are prerequisite to success in teaching? *The Nation's Schools, 6*, 60-64.

Barr, A. S., Torgerson, T. L., Johnson, C. E., Lyon, V. E., & Walvoord, A. C. (1935). The validity of certain instruments employed in the measurement of teaching ability. In H. M. Walker (Ed.), *The measurement of teaching efficiency*, Ch. IV. New York: MacMillan.

Boyce, A. C. (1915). Methods of measuring teachers' efficiency. *Fourteenth yearbook of the national society for the study of education, Part II. Bloomington, IL: Public School Publishing Co.*

Brookover, W. B. (1945). The relation of social factors to teaching ability. *Journal of Experimental Education, 13*, 191-205.

Campbell, D. T., & Erlebacher, A. (1971). How regression artifacts in quasi-experimental evaluations can mistakenly make compensatory education look harmful. In J. Hellmuth (Ed.), *The disadvantaged child, Vol. 3*. New York: Breimer/Mazel.

Gotham, R. E. (1945). Personality and teaching efficiency. *Journal of Experimental Education, 14*, 157-165.

Hellfritsch, A. G. (1945). A factor analysis of teacher abilities. *Journal of Experimental Education, 14*, 166-199.

Hill, C. W. (1921). The efficiency ratings of teachers. *Elementary School Journal, 21*, 438-443.

Jayne, C. D. (1945). A study of the relationship between teaching procedures and educational outcomes. *Journal of Experimental Education, 14*, 101-134.

Jones, R. D. (1946). The prediction of teaching efficiency from objective measures. *Journal of Experimental Education, 15*, 85-99.

LaDuke, C. V. (1945). The measurement of teaching ability. *Journal of Experimental Education, 14*, 75-100.

Lara, A. V. (1983). *Pupil ability as a moderator of correlations between teacher behavior patterns and pupil gains in reading and mathematics*. Unpublished doctoral dissertation, University of Virginia at Charlottesville.

Lins, L. J. (1946). The prediction of teaching efficiency. *Journal of Experimental Education, 15*, 2-60.

Medley, D. M., Coker, H., & Soar, R. S. (1984). *Measurement-based evaluation of teacher performance*. New York: Longman.

Medley, D. M., & Mitzel, H. E. (1959). Some behavioral correlates of teacher effectiveness, *Journal of Educational Psychology, 50*, 239-246.

Rugg, H. O. (1922). Is the rating of human character practicable? *Journal of Educational Psychology, 12*, 30-42.

Wells, F. L. (1907). A statistical study of literary merit. *Archives of Psychology No. 7*.

# SELF-TEST FOR TASK 1-A

**The Accuracy of Principals' Judgments of Teacher Performance**

**The Problem**

**The Procedures**

**The Method of Analysis**

**The Major Conclusion(s)**

# Reflective Thinking and Growth in Novices' Teaching Abilities

**JOAN P. GIPE**
University of New Orleans

**JANET C. RICHARDS**
The University of Southern Mississippi-Gulf Coast

ABSTRACT **Despite considerable differences in interpretations and agendas, reflective teaching programs are governed by the assumption that thoughtful and critically questioning novices will develop expertise in teaching abilities. However, there is no reported research that specifically examines prospective teachers' reflective thoughts in relation to improvement in teaching. This study examined the relationship between future teachers' reflections and growth in their teaching abilities in an early field placement. Data gathered over one semester from reflective journals and multiple observations were analyzed and descriptive statistics included. Results suggest that teacher preparation programs should foster reflective thinking as an important facet of growth in teaching abilities.**

The idea of reflection for prospective teachers is not new. However, recent favorable reports have helped place "reflective teaching" in vogue (Feiman-Nemser, 1990; Goodman, 1985; Zeichner, 1981-82). Teacher educators increasingly discuss the dimensions of reflection and teaching. Teacher education institutions purchase more reflective teaching materials than ever before (Gore, 1987). Supervisors now urge prospective teachers to think reflectively about their work. Novices in field placements are asked to keep journals, participate in seminars, or conduct mini-ethnographic studies. On a broader scale, some colleges are so committed to producing reflective teachers that comprehensive "inquiry-oriented" programs have been designed for that purpose (Korthagen, 1985; Korthagen & Verkuyl, 1987; Zeichner, 1981-82). Clearly, reflection "has become part of the [current] language of teacher education" (Gore, 1987, p. 33).

The scope and depth of university reflective program agendas differ considerably. Some education departments have tentatively begun to consider the merits of reflection; others have carefully monitored and continued to refine their programs for over 10 years.

Teacher education departments and teacher educators within those departments also differ in their interpretation of the widely used term *reflective teaching* (Beyer, 1984; Clift, Houston, & Pugach, 1990); that is, to think in a reflective way about pedagogical actions and concerns. Those considered to have a more "technocratic orientation" limit their interpretation of reflection to the teaching act (i.e., "teachers thinking about what happened, why it happened, and what else they could have done to reach their goal") (Gore, 1987, p. 36). The major focus of reflective thought is restricted to what occurs in classrooms.

Other inquiry-oriented pedagogists (Korthagen, 1985; Schon, 1987; Zeichner, 1981-82; Zeichner & Teitelbaum, 1982) expanded the definition of reflective teaching to include a critical "consideration of ethical, moral, and political principles" (Gore, 1987, p. 33). Reflective thoughts are extended beyond classroom walls to include "complexities inescapably linked with educational issues" (Hartnett & Naish, 1980, p. 269). That more radical and action-oriented perspective has the potential to stimulate educational reform. It urges both novices and supervisors to develop "habits of active, persistent, and careful examination of educational and social beliefs" (Zeichner, Liston, Mahlios, & Gomez, 1987, p. 5).

Educators also debate the most appropriate and effective ways to promote novices' reflective attitudes. Some educators believe that prospective teachers can objectively and analytically learn how to reflect about their teaching in a "complete and controlled clinical teaching experience" (Cruickshank, Holton, Fay, Williams, Kennedy, Myers, & Hough, 1981, part 1, p. 4). For example, one reflective teaching program requires novices to take turns teaching identical subject-matter lessons by following specifically stated manual guidelines. The lessons are taught to small groups of peers who then immediately reflect upon the variables that affected the instruction (Cruickshank & Applegate, 1981). Other experts emphatically reject the idea that prospective teachers can learn the skills of genuine reflective inquiry through a specific instructional method. Rather, it is the development of

*Address correspondence to Joan P. Gipe, Department of Curriculum & Instruction, University of New Orleans, New Orleans, LA 70148.*

positive and sincere attitudes about the merits of reflection that "constitute the basis of truly reflective action" (Zeichner, 1981-82, p. 6). Therefore, a wholesome attitude about reflection is as imperative as demonstrating reflective abilities.

Despite such widespread differences in program interpretations and agendas, activities designed to promote novices' reflective thinking are governed by a common assumption. The assumption links prospective teachers' reflective thoughts to their teaching behaviors (Cruickshank, 1984; Dewey, 1904, 1933; Zeichner, 1981-82). That is, prospective teachers who in some way reflect about their work, or who extend their reflections to include broader educational concerns, will improve upon their teaching abilities. Yet, that assumption cannot be taken for granted. Enthusiastic "claims about reflective teaching are in advance of any solid empirical evidence" (Gore, 1987, p. 35). Two related studies do suggest that novices in reflective teaching programs, as opposed to counterparts in traditional programs, are less anxious about teaching and more able to think and talk about teaching and learning (Holton & Nott, 1980; Williams & Kennedy, 1980). However, those studies have been critiqued as narrowly focused (Gore, 1987). Moreover, they do not demonstrate a link between reflective thinking and growth in novices' teaching competencies. The idea that thoughtful and critically questioning prospective teachers will demonstrate growth in abilities to devise and present appropriate lessons has not been documented. There is no reported research that specifically examines prospective teachers' reflective thoughts in relation to improved teaching abilities over the course of a semester. We conducted our study to formally explore that assumptive theme.

## Method

In this study, we used field research methodology, specifically analysis of reflective journals (Glaser & Strauss, 1967; Niemeyer & Moon, 1986; Yinger & Clark, 1981) and multiple observations (Medley & Mitzel, 1963; Meltzer, Petras, & Reynolds, 1975; Yonemura, 1987) coupled with some descriptive statistics. Research on journal writing supports the value of journals as a vehicle that promotes and documents reflective thinking (Erdman, 1983; Flower & Hayes, 1981; Gipe & Richards, 1990; Yinger & Clark, 1981). Observation produces insights about human behaviors that cannot be gained by any other method, and multiple observations substantially improve the reliability of behavioral data (Medley & Mitzel, 1963). Descriptive statistics quantify data so that comparisons can be more meaningfully interpreted (Gay, 1981).

The participants were 23 female elementary education majors enrolled in two reading/language arts methods courses designated as an early field experience. The novice teachers received 6 semester hours of credit for successful completion of the two courses. The semester's activities (e.g., lectures, demonstration lessons, and student teaching) were conducted at an inner-city school two mornings a week from 8:00 a.m. to 10:45 a.m.

The program, in its third semester at the elementary school, was guided by an emerging "inquiry-oriented" perspective. Seminar discussions focused upon novices' teaching concerns (e.g., why lessons went well or poorly, classroom management concerns, worries about a particular child, suggestions for future lessons). However, because of the supervisor's expanding goals for an inquiry-oriented program, existing school policies and practices also were considered in relation to socio/political realities. The topics, which arose naturally from the context of the field placement, included (a) who ultimately is responsible when a child receives overly harsh punishment in the classroom—teacher, principal, superintendent, school board, citizens; (b) who controls what occurs in classrooms; (c) the meaning of "the hidden curriculum"; and (d) the difficulty of continuing to teach with a holistic, child-centered instructional philosophy without collegial or supervisory support.

Dialogue journal activities were extensively used, although journal writing was not a graded course assignment. Each week, for 15 weeks, the prospective teachers wrote their thoughts and feelings about teaching in their journals. Each week the program supervisor read the journals and then wrote feedback comments designed to encourage the novices to reflect in their journals (e.g., "What could you have done differently?" "Who really is responsible when children fail? Please answer!" "How have your views about education changed since the beginning of the semester?" "I noted your problem. What were you thinking?" "Try to find the answer to your teaching dilemma within yourself and write the possible solutions in your journal.").

Following course lectures and demonstration lessons (8:00–9:00 a.m. each Monday and Wednesday), each prospective teacher worked with her own small groups of children in four different grade-level classrooms (prekindergarten through sixth grades, including gifted and learning disabled; two grade levels on Monday and two grade levels on Wednesday). Four novice teachers were assigned to the same classroom[1] during each 50-min time period (9:00–9:50 a.m. and 9:55–10:45 a.m.) throughout the semester, relieving the classroom teacher of teaching responsibilities during that time. Thus, each novice teacher prepared and taught four separate 50-min reading/language arts lessons weekly. The lessons were informally but attentively observed over the semester by the participating classroom teachers ($N = 16$) and were formally observed by the program supervisor.

### *Data Collection and Analysis*

Using a previously defined and agreed-upon criteria and rating scale (see Appendix B), the classroom teachers and the program supervisor independently evaluated the novices' teaching abilities at the end of the first month of the semester and during the last week of the semester. Each of 15 teachers rated their 4 novice teachers; the gifted classroom teacher rated 3 novices. Therefore, each novice was independently rated by four separate classroom teachers. Thus, the 23 prospective teachers each received five autonomous ratings of teaching ability at the end of the first month of the program and five autonomous ratings of teaching ability at the end of the program.

At the conclusion of the semester, the novices' initial five ratings for teaching ability were averaged and compared with their final teaching ability rating averages. For example, Novice 1 received end-of-first-month teaching ability ratings of 3, 2, 3, 2, 2, for an average of 2.4 (i.e., *occasionally* prepares and presents appropriate lessons). Final teaching ability ratings for Novice 1 were 4, 3, 4, 4, 4, for an average of 3.8 (i.e., *always* prepares and presents appropriate lessons). Table 1 contains results for all novices ($N$ = 23).

Additionally, two university supervisors who use dialogue journals on a regular basis with their own students, scored the novices' reflective journal statements. Each rater independently documented and scored the number of reflective statements per journal entry. Reflective statements were defined prior to scoring as statements within a single entry that demonstrated that novices were (a) attempting to make sense of their teaching experiences, questioning the status quo, considering future teaching alternatives, and coming to conclusions about students' abilities and behaviors (e.g., "I want to provide my students with a technique for analyzing and remembering. I've been wracking my brain trying to think of what I can do. Maybe we should write a rap song and put on a little play.") and (b) attempting to consider and question the impact of broader, socio-political concerns on classroom teachers' practices (e.g., "Why do they use fourth grade material with all fourth grade students? Who decides this?).

Nonreflective journal statements were defined as statements that provided the reader with a "recap" of the teaching session and omitted any attempts to brainstorm

**Table 1.—Novice Teachers' Initial and Final Teaching Ability Ratings—Range and Mean Number of Reflective Journal Statements**

| $n$ | Initial | Final | Range | Mean |
|---|---|---|---|---|
| 6 | 3.5–4.0 | 3.5–4.0 | 16–25 | 21.4 |
| 6 | 1.5-2.4 | 3.5–4.0 | 34–42 | 40.0 |
| 11 | 1.5-2.4 | 2.5-3.4 | 4–20 | 12.2 |

*Note*. No student received an initial teaching ability rating average in the 2.5-3.4 or 1.0-1.4 categories. 3.5–4.0 = *always* prepares and presents appropriate lessons; 2.5-3.4 = *usually* prepares and presents appropriate lessons; 1.5-2.4 = *occasionally* prepares and presents appropriate lessons; 1.0-1.4 = *never* prepares and presents appropriate lessons.

solutions to teaching dilemmas or questions about school policies. (See Appendix A for examples of journal entries reflecting teaching and broader educational concerns, as well as nonreflective journal entries.) Initial interrater reliability was .86. Differences in the two raters' opinions as to what they considered to be reflective statements were further resolved by discussion. Statements that were not agreed upon by both raters were excluded from the data analysis. The final analysis was a comparison of each novice's average teaching ability rating (end of first month and end of semester) with the number of reflective statements written in their reflective journals (see Table 1).

Six of the prospective teachers were rated at the end of the first month and at the end of the semester as "always prepares and presents appropriate lessons." The number of reflective journal statements written by those students for 15 journal entries ranged from 16 to 25 ($\bar{x}$ = 21.4). Six of the prospective teachers were rated at the end of the first month of the semester as occasionally and at the end of the semester as always prepares and presents appropriate lessons. The number of reflective journal statements written by the students for 15 journal entries ranged from 34 to 42 ($\bar{x}$ = 40). Eleven of the prospective teachers were rated at the end of the first month of the semester as occasionally and at the end of the semester as usually prepares and presents appropriate lessons. The number of reflective journal statements written by the students for 15 journal entries ranged from 4 to 20 ($\bar{x}$ = 12.2). Many of the reflections written by the 11 students had a negative and blaming tone (e.g., "Spare the rod and spoil the child with these kids!" "One boy in second grade started telling me he had a twin brother and baby brother. I found out later that this was a pack of lies!!!").

The 6 prospective teachers who were rated as improving the most in ability to prepare and present appropriate lessons (i.e., occasionally to always) wrote the largest number of reflective journal statements. Conversely, the 11 prospective teachers who were rated as least improved in ability to prepare and present appropriate lessons (i.e., occasionally to usually) wrote the fewest number of reflective journal statements. The 6 prospective teachers who were rated at the beginning and at the end of the semester as always prepares and presents appropriate lessons wrote a midrange number of reflective journal statements.

## Discussion

Research conducted within the classroom environment provides knowledge that cannot be gained by any other method. Yet, there are limitations to research conducted in a naturalistic setting. The dual role of the researcher as program supervisor and the idea that supervisors hold biases and beliefs that influence supervisory evaluations are acknowledged as possible limitations (Zeichner & Tabachnick, 1982). In this case, the researcher/supervisor was not neutral, but wholeheartedly believed in and encouraged a reflective teaching program. The classroom teachers' subjective views also must be acknowledged as possible limitations.

The use of an arbitrarily defined teacher ability rating scale (see Appendix B), may also be viewed as a limitation of this study. Further, the rating scale may not accurately depict equal increments of change in novices' teaching abilities (e.g., the distance between a rating of 2 to 3 may not equal the distance between a rating of 3 to 4). The rating scale represents an admittedly gross measure of novices' teaching abilities; nevertheless, it is one that classroom teachers serving as raters of novices' teaching abilities can easily use without infringing upon their already busy days. A more sensitive measure may have been able to document pedagogical growth in the novices who were rated initially, and throughout the semester, as always prepares and presents appropriate lessons. However, although there are sophisticated measures available for teacher evaluation, there are none that measure pedagogical growth. Such a measure is needed. One suggestion is to provide opportunities for preservice and inservice teachers to dialogue with each other about their professional development. In this way, a sensitive measure of novices' pedagogical growth may emerge.

Additionally, journal writing that requires writers to reflect through recollection may not sufficiently reveal every prospective teacher's sincerity, willingness, or ability to reflect about teaching. Personal preferences for privacy and individual choices for reflective modalities must be considered. For example, one student was queried about the sparsity of her writing. She responded in her journal, "I do reflect. But, I do it naturally . . . like in the shower or driving or going to sleep. You've got to have time to write and I'm working 32 hours per week." Nonetheless, all 23 novices did have the same number of opportunities to reflect (i.e., 15 journal entries), and all 23 subjects did attempt to reflect in their journals, but not all were successful (e.g., "I gave out their papers. I went over their mistakes. They all seemed to enjoy the lesson using semantic maps. That's about it. Is this what you mean by reflection?").

The goal of the study was to investigate the assumptive theme linking prospective teachers' reflective thinking and improvement in teaching abilities. Although it is premature to conclude that the more that prospective teachers reflect about their work, the more their teaching abilities will improve, the results of the study suggest that the assumptive theme that links prospective teachers' reflective thinking to their teaching is an appropriate assumption. The first formal connection between future teachers' reflections and improvements in their teaching ability suggests that "teacher preparation should foster reflective capacities" (Doyle, 1990, p. 6). Teacher educators who are tentatively contemplating the merits of a reflective program may now wish to initiate such agendas.

The results also suggest that prospective teachers' reflections can help supervisors to analyze whether novices' classroom experiences provide the right conditions for growth (Maslow, 1968) and to prescribe appropriate contexts for novices' future field placements. For example, as indicated by their journals, the prospective teachers who were always unanimously rated high in teaching ability apparently did not feel compelled to reflect a great deal about their teaching (see Table 1). They did not have to worry about solving professional problems such as pondering alternatives to instruction. When they were urged to reflect more, one of the 6 highly rated students confidently wrote, "I don't need to reflect or worry about my work. I know that things will go OK and if they don't, I make them turn out OK." A second placement that provides some frustrations and dissonance may force the 6 pedagogically competent novices to reflect upon educational dilemmas to resolve uncertainties and, therefore, be "pulled into a new level of growth" (Bolin, 1987, p. 8).

Similarly, the accomplishments of the 6 novice teachers who increased their teaching ability the most by the end of the semester have more meaning when their journal reflections are considered. The 6 future teachers reflected considerably about their work, and they achieved substantial professional growth. Furthermore, the small amount and mainly negative tone of the reflections written by the 11 prospective teachers who were rated as improving the least in teaching abilities indicates that those students may need a second, more structured, nonthreatening field placement with nurturing, supportive supervision to advance professionally. There is a relationship between safety and growth; "Assured safety permits higher needs and impulses to emerge and to grow towards mastery" (Maslow, 1968, p. 49).

Finally, results of this study highlight the importance of the context of the field placement with respect to promoting prospective teachers' reflections about teaching. A nonchallenging field experience may provide few opportunities for reflective thought, because there are few problems to solve. An overly threatening field placement may promote negativism and stagnation. Reflection becomes subordinate to survival concerns. A field placement that offers moderate amounts of ambiguity and dissonance (Bolin, 1987; Hollingsworth, 1989) may provide opportunities for problem solving through reflection and thereby enhance professional growth.

## APPENDIX A

*Examples of Reflective Journal Statements Depicting Novices' Teaching Concerns*

*Journal No. 5*

I think the children responded to these statements because it called attention to themselves. When I used declarative statements the children didn't respond. It seemed that by giving them a direct statement they believed that what I said was truth. When I used "wait time" one girl thought I was mad. They are too young and too inexperienced to understand that I wanted them to elaborate. Now I know that I have to guide them through a discussion.

*Journal No. 12*

I don't know if I can take this kind of pain. I feel a certain closeness with my group and now . . . also a sadness. We all know that we'll probably never see one another again. I'm really going to miss them. Teachers are special people, aren't they? They know things about kids that no one else could know.

*Journal No. 21*

I still don't see why everyone thinks that Sam [fictitious name] is such a good teacher. His class seems kind of dull to me. I think visuals in upper levels would help generate interest in the topics and stimulate a desire to learn. Why doesn't he let his students decorate the class with their work?

*Journal No. 23*

One student in particular was reluctant to get involved. So I just kept including her in the lesson—calling on her to take her turn, etc. She rolled her eyes, etc. but participated nonetheless. I'm concerned about why she was so lethargic and sleepy. It was almost as if she were drugged. I have to find out if this is her usual state or not. Maybe she's having personal troubles that lead to her behavior. It concerns me.

*Examples of Reflective Journal Statements Depicting Novices' Broader Educational Concerns*

*Journal No. 2*

I'm shocked! What a day! Why am I so shocked? I don't know. I guess I just didn't expect the kids to be so casual. Are all schools in the U.S. this way now? How did things change since I was in elementary school?

*Journal No. 11*

Guess what? I have had my eyes opened and I still want to teach. I love it! I guess sometimes we get so involved with just teaching that we don't stop to think clearly. When I think in this journal I think how much I've learned about teaching. I have a long way to go, but now I know that some teachers and some schools don't treat kids like real people. The worst part is I don't think anyone cares.

*Journal No. 19*

One problem is that these parents need to help their kids more by making sure they eat breakfast and get to bed on time. Another problem is that the kindergarten kids have to do too much paper work and ditto sheets. Another thing . . . Hannah [fictitious name] says she can't even teach the kids what she knows they need because she'll get into trouble if she doesn't follow the curriculum. Do you really have to follow a curriculum if it's not right for the kids?

*Examples of Nonreflective Journal Statements*

*Journal No. 3*

At first when I arrived there wasn't a soul in sight. The building looked old and broken down and it was very HOT! Soon after, people started coming so I went inside. You began our lecture and I learned different auding [listening] strategies to use with children. Thanks!

*Journal No. 6*

In my sixth grade group I had two new students. They hadn't been there before due to absences. There was a constant chatter among the people in my group. I asked one of them to leave the group. He couldn't be quiet and didn't want to participate in the group activity. I guess that's the way it is here. The kids have a lot of freedom.

*Journal No. 14*

The first thing they did was to read and write in their dialogue journals. After writing in their journals they made the final changes in their stories for the creative book. The stories are great! The rest of the time was spent on illustrating the books. They have to be completed by March 20th. I let them decide which parts they wanted to illustrate and then they were on their own. Everything's going fine!

*Journal No. 16*

I did teacher dictation and they seemed to like that. We did seven sentences and they all participated, even the ones I had put out of the group would listen and follow along. I hope that was okay? After we did this I read *The King Who Rained*, by Fred Gwynn, and I explained it as I went through it. As usual, it all is going well!

## APPENDIX B

*Criteria for Rating Prospective Teachers' Abilities to Prepare and Present Appropriate Reading/Language Arts Lessons*

a. Creates and uses teacher-made games and learning aids.
b. Presents reading/language arts topics commensurate with children's cognitive development, instructional needs, and interests.
c. Uses current research-based reading/language arts instructional strategies.*

**Examples of Current Research-Based Reading/Language Arts Instructional Strategies*

- Takes individual or group dictation.
- Assists children in creating puppet plays and drama activities.
- Encourages creative bookmaking.
- Teaches subprocesses of the writing process (e.g., planning, composing, revising, evaluating compositions).
- Teaches reading comprehension (e.g., uses cloze/maze procedures, directed reading-thinking activities, semantic mapping).
- Expands children's vocabularies and cognitive development through group discussions, experiential activities, and vicarious experiences.

*Teaching Ability Rating Scale*

4 = *Always* prepares and presents appropriate lessons.
3 = *Usually* prepares and presents appropriate lessons.
2 = *Occasionally* prepares and presents appropriate lessons.
1 = *Never* prepares and presents appropriate lessons.

## NOTE

The gifted classroom received only 3 novice teachers because fewer numbers of children needed to be accommodated. Therefore, five classrooms received 4 novice teachers, and one classroom received 3 novices, totalling 23 novice teachers.

## REFERENCES


Beyer, L. (1984). Field experience, ideology, and the development of critical reflectivity. *Journal of Teacher Education, 35*(3), 36–41.

Bolin, F. (1987, April). *Students' conceptions of teaching as revealed in preservice journals.* Paper presented at the annual meeting of the American Educational Research Association. Washington, DC.

Clift, R., Houston, W. R., & Pugach, M. (Eds.) (1990). Encouraging reflective practice in education: An analysis of issues and programs. New York: Teachers College Press.

Cruickshank, D. (1984). *Helping teachers achieve wisdom.* Unpublished manuscript. The Ohio State University, College of Education, Columbus, OH.

Cruickshank, D., & Applegate, J. (1981). Reflective teaching as a strategy for teacher growth. *Educational Leadership, 38*(7), 553-554.

Cruickshank, D., Holton, J., Fay, D., Williams, J., Kennedy, J., Myers, B., & Hough, J. (1981). *Reflective teaching*. Bloomington, IN: Phi Delta Kappa.

Dewey, J. (1904). The relation of theory to practice in education. In C. A. McMurray (Ed.), *The relation of theory to practice in the education of teachers* (Third Yearbook of the National Society for the Study of Education, Part 1, pp. 9-30). Bloomington, IL: Public School Publishing.

Dewey, J. (1933). *How we think: A restatement of the relation of reflective thinking to the educational process.* Boston: D. C. Heath.

Doyle, W. (1990). Themes in teacher education research. In W. R. Houston, M. Haberman, & J. Sikula (Eds.), *Handbook of research on teacher education* (pp. 3-24). New York: Macmillan.

Erdman, J. (1983). Assessing the purposes of early field placement programs. *Journal of Teacher Education, 34*, 27-31.

Feiman-Nemser, S. (1990). Teacher preparation: Structural and conceptual alternatives. In W. R. Houston, M. Haberman, & J. Sikula (Eds.), *Handbook of research on teacher education* (pp. 212-223). New York: Macmillan.

Flower, L., & Hayes, J. (1981). A cognitive process theory of writing. *College Composition and Communication, 32*, 365-387.

Gay, L. (1981). *Educational research* (2nd ed.). Columbus, OH: Charles E. Merrill.

Gipe, J. P., & Richards, J. C. (1990, Spring). Promoting reflection about reading instruction through journaling. *Journal of Reading Education, 15*(3), 6-13.

Glaser, B., & Strauss, A. (1967). The discovery of grounded theory: Strategies for qualitative research. Chicago: Aldine.

Goodman, J. (1985). What students learn from early field experiences: A case study and critical analysis. *Journal of Teacher Education, 36*(6), 42-48.

Gore, J. (1987). Reflecting on reflective teaching. *Journal of Teacher Education, 38*(2), 33-39.

Harnett, A., & Naish, M. (1980). Technicians or social bandits? Some moral and political issues in the education of teachers. In P. Woods (Ed.), *Teacher strategies* (pp. 225-274). London: Croom Helm.

Hollingsworth, S. (1989). Prior beliefs and cognitive change in learning to teach. *American Educational Research Journal, 26*, 160-189.

Holton, J., & Nott, D. (1980, April). *The experimental effects of reflective teaching on preservice teachers' ability to think and talk critically about teaching and learning.* Paper presented at the annual meeting of the American Educational Research Association, Boston, MA.

Korthagen, F. (1985). Reflective teaching and preservice teacher education in the Netherlands. *Journal of Teacher Education, 36*(5), 11-15.

Korthagen, F., & Verkuyl, H. (1987, April). *Supply and demand: Towards differentiation in teacher education, based on differences in learning orientations.* Paper presented at the annual meeting of the American Educational Research Association, Washington, DC.

Maslow, A. (1968). *Toward a psychology of being.* New York: Van Nostrand Reinhold.

Medley, D., & Mitzel, H. (1963). Measuring classroom behavior by systematic observation. In N. Gage (Ed.), *Handbook of research on teaching* (pp. 247-328). Chicago: Rand McNally.

Meltzer, B., Petras, J., & Reynolds, L. (1975). *Symbolic interactionism: Genesis, varieties and criticism.* London: Routledge and Kegan Paul.

Neimeyer, R, & Moon, A. (1986, April). *Researching decision-making in the supervision of student teachers.* Paper presented at the annual meeting of the American Educational Research Association, San Francisco.

Schon, D. (1987). *Educating the reflective practitioner.* San Francisco: Jossey-Bass.

Williams, F., & Kennedy, J. (1980, April). *The effects of reflective teaching relative to promoting attitudinal change.* Paper presented at the annual meeting of the American Educational Research Association, Boston, MA.

Yinger, R., & Clark, C. (1981). *Reflective journal writing: Theory and practice* (IRT Occasional Paper No. 50). East Lansing, MI: Institute for Research on Teaching, Michigan State University.

Yonemura, M. (1987). *A teacher at work: Professional development and the early childhood educator.* New York: Teachers College Press.

Zeichner, K. (1981-82). Reflective teaching and field-based experience in teacher education. *Interchange, 12*, 1-22.

Zeichner, K., Liston, D., Mahlios, M., & Gomez, M. (1987, April). *The structure and goals of a student teaching program and the character and quality of supervisory discourse.* Paper presented at the annual meeting of the American Educational Research Association, Washington, DC.

Zeichner, K., & Tabachnick, B. (1982). The belief systems of university supervisors in an elementary student-teaching program. *Journal of Education for Teaching, 8*, 34-54.

Zeichner, K., & Teitelbaum, K. (1982). Personalized and inquiry-oriented teacher education: An analysis of two approaches to the development of curriculum for field-based experience. *Journal of Education for Teaching, 8*, 95-117.

# SELF-TEST FOR TASK 1-A

## Reflective Thinking and Growth in Novices' Teaching Abilities

**The Problem**

**The Procedures**

**The Method of Analysis**

**The Major Conclusion(s)**

# Classroom Behavior of Good and Poor Readers

**BARBARA B. WASSON**
**PAUL L. BEARE**
**JOHN B. WASSON**
**Moorhead State University**

ABSTRACT **The purpose of this study was to investigate objectively observable categories of behavior for good and poor readers in classroom settings. Seven specific observable behaviors of 3 good and 3 poor readers from each of three regular classrooms at each of six grade levels were viewed under natural classroom conditions. Trained observers recorded student behavior for 30 min a day for 10 days. A two-way analysis of variance procedure was used in data analysis. Results indicated that poor readers did not differ from good readers in starting to work on assignments, having necessary materials available, making unacceptable noise, being out of place, or making unacceptable contact with other persons or their property. Poor readers, however, were off task more and volunteered less than good readers did. The results were interpreted to suggest that poor readers could be viewed as uninvolved students. Instructional suggestions are given.**

Researchers have written that poor readers and good readers behave differently. In an early review of clinically observed characteristics of poor readers, Robinson (1946) included restlessness, introversive or withdrawal tendencies, inadequate school relations, and conscious self-control bordering on rigidity. Harris and Sipay (1985) cited expressed hostility, negative emotional response to reading, lack of effort, passivity, distractibility or restlessness, and lack of attentive concentration as characteristics of poor readers.

Poor readers, in general, although not in every case, have been characterized as tending to demonstrate maladaptive behavior (Gentile & McMillan, 1987; Jorm, Share, Matthews, & MacClean, 1985). Based on a substantial review of research, Gentile and McMillan characterized the behavior of poor readers as ranging from anger and aggression to avoidance and apprehension.

Classroom behavior has been shown to be highly related to reading achievement among first- and second-grade children (Jorm et al., 1985; McMichael, 1979; Swanson, 1984). On the other hand, Zigmond, Kerr, and Schaeffer (1988) found that the classroom behavior of learning-disabled adolescents enrolled in Grades 1 through 11 is not significantly different from the behavior of their non-learning-disabled peers. Among the behaviors studied were on-task behavior, disruptive behavior, and volunteering comments.

Confusion arises about behavioral characteristics of good and poor readers when clinically derived subjective descriptions are compared with objectively measured classroom behavior and when the behavior of primary children is compared with that of adolescents.

The present research attempts to provide consistency by investigating a single set of objectively observable behaviors of both good and poor readers in classroom settings from Grades 1 through 11.

## Method

### *Subjects*

The subjects were 108 students enrolled in regular classes from Grades 1, 3, 5, 7, 9, and 11. Classrooms were selected from public schools in a midsized (population 65,000) city in the north central United States.

We chose subjects who were the 3 best and the 3 worst readers in each of three classrooms at each of six grade levels. The relative standing of students was determined by examining the latest standardized reading achievement test scores for each student in each class, except for first-grade students, for whom kindergarten teachers' ratings were used as the basis for selection. The 3 students with the highest and the 3 students with the lowest reading achievement scores became subjects. The fourth highest and the fourth lowest students became alternates if any of the original choices were absent on the first day of observation.

At each of six grade levels, we chose a total of 9 good readers and 9 poor readers from three classrooms. Selection thus resulted in the total of 108 students from 18

*Address correspondence to Barbara B. Wasson, Department of Education, Moorhead State University, Moorhead, MN 56560.*

classrooms, 54 categorized as good and 54 categorized as poor readers. The final sample was composed of 106 originally chosen subjects and 2 alternates.

*Procedure*

Based on a review of literature that specified classroom behaviors associated with good as opposed to poor readers (Gentile & McMillan, 1987; Jorm et al., 1985; McMichael, 1979; Zigmond, Kerr, & Schaeffer, 1988), discussion with classroom teachers, and review of methods for objectively observing student behavior in classroom settings (Deno, 1980; Grambrell, Wilson, & Gantt, 1981; Hoge, 1985; Hoge & Luce, 1979), we chose specific behaviors that seemed likely to differentiate good from poor readers. We observed these specific behaviors in classrooms on a trial basis to ensure that they could be consistently identified. From the original set of specific behaviors, we chose seven that could be consistently identified and precisely defined. Behavioral definitions were refined through pilot sessions performed in classrooms not used in the actual research. Pilot sessions continued until a reliability of 90% was attained by independent observers recording the behavior of the same students at the same time. The behaviors and definitions used in the research follow:

1. *Seconds to start*—number of seconds from the beginning of an activity, as indicated by the teacher, until the student is first on task. Duration recording, 5-min maximum. *First on task*—materials are out and the student is in place, listening to the teacher, making eye contact with the appropriate stimuli, and writing, or has pencil poised, ready to write. The student is not on task when looking for materials.
2. *Materials missing*—number of materials needed for instruction that a student is missing, based on a list obtained from the teacher prior to the observation.

The following five behaviors were recorded using an interval method—one mark for 20-s interval during which the behavior occurred.

3. *Noise*—any sounds created by the student that may distract either another student (or students) or the teacher from the business at hand. The noise may be generated vocally (including talk outs or unintelligible sounds) or nonvocally (tapping a pencil or snapping fingers). Incidentally produced noises (chair squeaks, etc.) are excluded.
4. *Out of place*—any movement beyond the either explicitly or implicitly defined boundaries in which the student is allowed movement. If the student is doing desk work, then movement of any sort out of the seat is out of place. If the student is working with a group, then leaving the group is out of place.
5. *Physical contact or destruction*—any unacceptable contact with another person or another person's property. Kicking, hitting, pushing, tearing, breaking, and taking are categorized as physical contact or destruction.
6. *Off task*—any movement off a prescribed activity that does not fall into one of the three previously defined categories. Looking around, staring into space, doodling, or any observable movement off the task at hand is included.
7. *Volunteering*—deliberately volunteering to answer questions or verbally participate in class, including raising a hand to answer or speaking out to answer, even without permission.

We gathered research data by observing each classroom for 30 min a day for 10 days. To prevent experimenter bias, we were not told which students were poor readers, but only which 6 students to observe.

We did not observe reading classes because of a lack of secondary-level reading classes and because the behavior that characterizes poor readers, according to the literature, is more general than a simple reaction to a reading class. Instead, social studies classes, which require students to apply reading skills, were selected for observation. When certain elementary classroom teachers did not teach clearly defined social studies lessons, we substituted language arts lessons.

Behavioral observation began at the start of each day's lesson. Prior to the start of the lesson, the classroom teacher supplied the trained observer with a list of materials that the children needed for the lesson. The teacher also indicated to the observer when the lesson began. The observer than measured the length of time until each student was first on task. The maximum time allotted was 5 min. After 5 min elapsed, the observer recorded materials missing, that is, materials the student did not have that were required for the lesson. Length of time until each student was first on task and materials missing were recorded for each student each day.

The remaining five categories of behavior listed above as numbers 3 through 7 were measured on a rotating interval basis. We observed each student, in turn, for 20 s, and he or she could receive a mark any time during the 20-s interval. Following this procedure, we observed each student for 20 s every 2 min, and he or she could receive a score of from 0 to 15 for noise, out of place, physical contact, off task, or volunteering each day.

**Results**

We analyzed the data by using a two-way analysis of variance (ANOVA) procedure. Rate of behavior was the dependent variable, and good versus poor reader groups and grade level were the two independent variables.

The mean scores for each of the seven measured behaviors are reported by reader group in Table 1 and by grade level in Table 2. Table 2 does not break down grade level by good and poor readers because no significant interactions were found by grade level and reading achievement. Analysis of variance for each of the behaviors yielded the following results:

1. *Seconds to start*—No difference was found between good and poor readers. Although significant differences were found between grade levels, $F(5, 107) = 6.337, p < .05$, they made little practical difference, because most students at every grade level started from ½ to 1 min after the beginning of the lesson.

2. *Materials missing*—No differences were found between good and poor readers or between grade levels. There were almost no missing materials throughout the duration of the study.

3. *Noise*—Incidents of unacceptable distracting noise were infrequent. No difference was found between good and poor readers or between grade levels.

4. *Out of place*—No difference was found between good and poor readers. There were significant grade level differences, $F(5, 107) = 5.851, p < .05$. Post hoc analysis indicated that 1st- and 3rd-grade children were out of place significantly more often than were 5th-, 7th-, 9th-, and 11th-grade students.

5. *Physical contact or destruction*—Incidents of physical contact or destruction were infrequent. No difference was found between good and poor readers or between grade levels.

6. *Off task*—Much off-task behavior was observed, almost 6 min (median) for the entire group of 108 students per 30-min observation. Poor readers were off task significantly more often than good readers, $F(1, 107) = 7.925, p < .05$. Seventh-grade students were significantly less off task, $F(5, 107) = 18.01, p < .05$, than were students from other grades.

7. *Volunteering*—Significant differences were found between good and poor readers in deliberately volunteering information, $F(1, 107) = 14.99, p < .05$. Students from Grade 5 and above volunteered less than did those from Grades 1 and 3.

## Discussion

We found no differences between good and poor readers in starting to work on assignments, having necessary materials available, making unacceptable noise, being out of place, or making unacceptable contact with other persons or their property. In these respects, poor readers did not differ from good readers when they were systemactically observed in regular classroom situations that involved application of reading, but not direct instruction in reading.

On the other hand, we found significant differences between good and poor readers in attending to instructional tasks. Similar to findings reported by Grambrell, Wilson, and Gantt (1981), poor readers attended less. Significant differences also were found in volunteering to participate verbally in class. Poor readers volunteered less.

**Table 1.—Mean Scores for Seven Behaviors Exhibited by 54 Good and 54 Poor Readers Over 10 Days of Observation**

| Group | Behavior | | | | | | |
|---|---|---|---|---|---|---|---|
| | Seconds to start | Materials missing[a] | Noise[b] | Out of place[b] | Physical contact[b] | Off task[b] | Volunteers[b] |
| Poor reader | 51 | .00 | 1.67 | .31 | .02 | 6.63 | 1.45 |
| Good reader | 43 | .02 | 1.50 | .32 | .00 | 5.51 | 2.47 |

*Note.* $p < .05$ pertains to both off-task and volunteering behavior.
[a]Number of missing objects. [b]Number of intervals during which behavior occurs (out of 15 possible).

**Table 2.—Mean Scores for Seven Behaviors Exhibited by 18 Subjects at Each of Six Grade Levels Over 10 Days of Observation**

| Grade | Behavior totals | | | | | | |
|---|---|---|---|---|---|---|---|
| | Seconds to start | Materials missing[a] | Noise[b] | Out of place[b] | Physical contact[b] | Off task[b] | Volunteers[b] |
| 1 | 42 | .0 | 2.1 | .7 | 0 | 4.8 | 3.6 |
| 1 | 42 | .0 | 2.1 | .7 | 0 | 4.8 | 3.6 |
| 3 | 63 | .0 | 0.9 | .7 | 0 | 7.3 | 2.8 |
| 5 | 68 | .0 | 1.3 | .1 | 0 | 8.5 | 1.7 |
| 7 | 26 | .0 | 1.0 | .1 | 0 | 2.8 | 1.9 |
| 9 | 25 | .1 | 1.9 | .3 | 0 | 5.8 | 1.0 |
| 11 | 59 | .0 | 2.3 | .1 | 0 | 7.3 | 0.8 |

[a]Number of missing objects. [b]Number of intervals during which behavior occurs (out of 15 possible).

This research suggests that in the regular classroom, at all grade levels observed, poor readers did not demonstrate disruptive or noncompliant behaviors that interfered with learning any more than did good readers. In terms of active participation in learning, however, a difference did appear to exist. The poor readers were less engaged and involved than good readers and also inferior in responsiveness and attentive learning.

Gentile and McMillan (1987) made suggestions specifically for poor readers who are uninvolved in learning. The authors suggested that the teachers should emphasize drawing these students out and focusing them on instructional tasks. The teachers should directly prompt and cue unengaged, inattentive learners, guiding them back to academic tasks. Unresponsive learners should be, in a supportive manner, directly requested to respond. The teachers should provide emotional and instructional support designed to generate students' willingness to try.

Students will be more willing to respond when teachers do not embarrass them over incorrect responses and do not give them text materials that are too difficult (Wilson, 1985, pp. 183-198). Bristow (1985) recommended that, to encourage active participation, poor readers must encounter instructional situations in which their efforts can make a difference. In addition, because poor readers tend to perceive themselves as less successful than they are, teachers should honestly and accurately expose the readers' successes.

Teachers who want to help poor readers participate more actively in the classroom should directly, but supportively, ask them to respond, ensure that the classroom learning environment permits participation to result in success, and commend poor readers directly and specifically for their responses and for their successes.

## REFERENCES


Bristow, P. S. (1985). Are poor readers passive readers? Some evidence, possible explanations, and potential solutions. *The Reading Teacher, 39*, 318-325.

Deno, S. L. (1980). Direct observation approach to measuring classroom behavior. *Exceptional Children, 47*, 396-399.

Gentile, L. M., & McMillan, M. M. (1987). *Stress and reading difficulties: Research, assessment, intervention*. Newark, DE: International Reading Association.

Grambrell, L. B., Wilson, R. M., & Gantt, W. N. (1981). Classroom observations of task-attending behaviors of good and poor readers. *Journal of Educational Research, 74*, 400-404.

Harris, A. J., & Sipay, E. R. (1985). *How to increase reading ability* (8th ed.). New York: Longman.

Hoge, R. D. (1985). The validity of direct observation measures of pupil classroom behavior. *Review of Educational Research, 55*, 469-483.

Hoge, R. D., & Luce, S. (1979). Predicting academic achievement from classroom behavior. *Review of Educational Research, 49*, 479-496.

Jorm, A. F., Share, D. L., Matthews, R., & MacClean, R. (1985). Behavior problems in specific reading retarded and general reading backward children: A longitudinal study. *Journal of Child Psychology & Psychiatry & Allied Disciplines, 27*, 33-43.

McMichael, P. (1979). The hen or the egg? Which comes first—Antisocial emotional disorders or reading ability? *British Journal of Educational Psychology, 49*, 226-238.

Robinson, H. M. (1946). *Why pupils fail in reading*. Chicago: University of Chicago Press.

Swanson, B. B. (1984). The relationship of first graders' self-report and direct observational attitude scores to reading achievement. *Reading Improvement, 21*, 170.

Wilson, R. M. (1985). *Diagnostic reading for classroom and clinic* (5th ed.). Columbus, OH: Merrill.

Zigmond, N., Kerr, M. M., & Schaeffer, A. (1988). Behavior patterns of learning disabled and non-learning-disabled adolescents in high school academic classes. *Remedial and Special Education, 9*(2), 6-11.

# SELF-TEST FOR TASK 1-A

## Classroom Behavior of Good and Poor Readers

**The Problem**

**The Procedures**

**The Method of Analysis**

**The Major Conclusion(s)**

**Task 1-B**

Given reprints of three research studies, classify each as historical, qualitative, descriptive, correlational, causal-comparative, or experimental research and state the characteristics of each study which support the classification chosen.

Part One in your text includes a number of examples for each of the types of research. Reread them and see if you can come up with some examples of your own. After you have generated some examples, ask yourself the questions presented within the section of Part One entitled Guidelines for Classification. If the answers to those questions suggest that each example does indeed represent the method of research you intended it to represent, you are in business (that means you are probably ready for Task 1-B). As a self-test, classify by type the preceding research reports; use the form which follows. If all your choices and reasons agree with the Suggested Responses, you are <u>definitely</u> ready for Task 1-B. If you miss one, make sure you understand why you were in error. If you miss several, and especially if you do not understand why, see your instructor.

## SELF-TEST FOR TASK 1-B

**Reading Time in School: Effect on Fourth Graders' Performance on a Criterion-Referenced Comprehension Test**

**Type:**______________________________

**Reasons:**______________________________

______________________________

______________________________

______________________________

______________________________

**Teachers' Use of Homework in High Schools**

**Type:**______________________________

**Reasons:**______________________________

______________________________

______________________________

______________________________

______________________________

**The Accuracy of Principals' Judgments of Teacher Performance**

**Type:**______________________________

**Reasons:**______________________________

______________________________

______________________________

______________________________

______________________________

**Reflective Thinking and Growth in Novices' Teaching Abilities**

**Type:**________________________________________

**Reasons:**______________________________________

______________________________________________

______________________________________________

______________________________________________

______________________________________________

**Classroom Behavior of Good and Poor Readers**

**Type:**________________________________________

**Reasons:**______________________________________

______________________________________________

______________________________________________

______________________________________________

______________________________________________

# PART TWO

## RESEARCH PROBLEMS

### Exercises

**Exercise II-1**

In each item below, you are given a brief description of subjects (Ss), an independent variable (X), and a dependent variable (Y). For each item, write a directional research hypothesis.

1. Ss = at-risk eighth graders
   X = self-esteem course
   Y = grade point average

   ______________________________________________

   ______________________________________________

   ______________________________________________

   ______________________________________________

2. Ss = college-level introductory psychology students
   X = type of testing (short-answer versus multiple choice)
   Y = retention of psychological concepts and principles

   ______________________________________________

   ______________________________________________

   ______________________________________________

   ______________________________________________

3. Ss = public school students
   X = high school graduation
   Y = income at age 25

   ______________________________________________

   ______________________________________________

   ______________________________________________

   ______________________________________________

4. Ss = third-grade students
   X = use of manipulative materials
   Y = mathematical achievement

5. Ss = tenth-grade biology students
   X = type of lab (hands-on dissection versus model manipulation)
   Y = attitudes toward biology

**Exercise II-2**

For each item in Exercise II-1, write a null hypothesis.

1.

2.

3.

4.

5.

# PART TWO

## RESEARCH PROBLEMS

### Objectives Example

**Objectives**

1. Make a list of at least three educational problems for which you would be interested in conducting a research study.

2. Select one of the problems; identify 10 - 15 references which directly relate to the selected problem. (See text for list of suggested sources.)

3. Read and abstract the references you have listed.

4. Formulate at least one testable hypothesis for your problem.

The Objectives for Part Two (Chapter 2) are different in that, unlike the Objectives for other chapters, their achievement is assessed by evaluating the product, not by a test. Since you may be required to submit the related work to your instructor, an example is provided to guide you. This example was written by S. J. Calderin, whose Task 2 is presented as an example in the text. Note that not all of the references in the following example were used in the Task 2 paper.

You will notice that some of the abstracts are in quotation marks, and some are not. If the abstract published with an article contained all necessary information, i.e., was a good abstract, it was used as is. If an article did not have an abstract, or if the given abstract lacked relevant information, an acceptable one was written. If you are not sure if this strategy is allowed by your instructor, check; she or he may prefer that all abstracts be written by you.

Effects of Multimedia on the Achievement
of Tenth-Grade Biology Students

Tentative Hypothesis: Tenth-grade biology students whose teachers use multimedia as part of their instructional technique will achieve at a higher standard than tenth-grade biology students whose teachers do not use multimedia.

A. EDUCATION INDEX

Kneedler, P. E. (1993). California adopts multimedia science program. Technological Horizons in Education Journal, 20(70), 73-76.

This article describes the evolution of "Science 2000," a non-textbook multimedia science program adopted by the California State Board of Education for the seventh grade. The program is flexible, allowing the teachers to design lessons to include their own experiences and to meet the particular learning styles of their students. Videodiscs and other media provide students with data to carry out a scientific investigation.

B. READERS' GUIDE TO PERIODICAL LITERATURE

Corcoran, E. (1989). Show and Tell: Hypermedia turns information into a multisensory event. Scientific American, 261, 72,74.

This article explains what is meant by hypermedia and describes some of the ways it can be used, one of which is classroom instruction. Hypermedia organizes and links information so that it can be retrieved in an assortment of media such as text, pictures, video clips and sound. The benefits of hypermedia, such as its ease of use, are weighed against the critics' claim that it is gimmicky and does not impart knowledge.

C. DISSERTATION ABSTRACT INTERNATIONAL

Chagas, I. (1993). Teachers as innovators: A case study of implementing the interactive videodisc in a middle school science program. Dissertation Abstract International, 53, 4268A (University Microfilms No. DA9311115)

"The purpose of this study was twofold: first, to provide an extensive and detailed description of two middle school science teachers implementing Interactive Videodisc (IVD) in their sixth-grade classes, and second, to interpret the data in terms of the role played by the IVD as a vehicle for educational change. The characteristics of the school emerged as an important factor in explaining why the two teachers engaged in such an innovative process. The school's philosophy supported innovation and it was a 'computer-experienced school' in which computers were regarded as tools to facilitate the work of both students and faculty. Several constraints on the use of the IVD were detected: difficulties in integrating the content of the selected program with the unit under study, difficulties in justifying the activity to students in such a way that they approached it seriously, and difficulties in organizing the classroom to accommodate the characteristics of IVD. The IVD worked as an additional strategy to encourage students' active participation in their own learning and not as a substitute for any strategy commonly used in science teaching. The students engaged in lively interactions that were not observed in other activities. Conclusions were organized according to three themes identified during the study: teachers as innovators, peer collaboration, and IDV in the classroom. Implications were discussed according to the generalizability for teacher training programs."

D. PSYCHOLOGICAL ABSTRACTS

Leonard, W.H. (1989) A comparison of student reaction to biology instruction by interactive videodisc or conventional laboratory. Journal of Research in Science Teaching, 26, 95-104.

"This study was designed to learn if university students perceived an interactive computer/videodisc learning system to represent a viable alternative to (or extension of) the conventional laboratory for learning biology skills and concepts normally taught under classroom laboratory conditions. Students frequently remarked that videodisc instruction gave more experimental and procedural options and more efficient use of instructional time than did the conventional laboratory mode. These two results are consistent with past CAI research. Students found the two approaches to be equivalent to conventional laboratory instruction in the area of general interest, understanding of basic principles, help on examinations, and attitude toward science. The student-opinion data in this study do not suggest that interactive videodisc technology serve as a substitute to the 'wet' laboratory experience, but that this medium may enrich the spectrum of educational experiences usually not possible in typical classroom settings."

Sherwood, R.D., Kinzer, C.K., Bransford, J.D., & Franks, J.J. (1987). Some benefits of creating macro-contexts for science instruction: Initial findings. Journal of Research in Science Training, 24, 417-435.

"Our goal in this paper is to present initial data indicating that learning can be enhanced when information is presented in the context of video-based macro-contexts that illustrate how science information can be used to solve meaningful problems. The experiments show positive results through simple uses technology." A videodisc was used to show segments of a film to one group after they had a lecture on spiders, while another group only received the lecture. "The results suggest that more sophisticated uses of technology, especially computer-controlled interactive videodisc technology, would have even greater benefits on comprehension and learning in science."

E. RESOURCES IN EDUCATION

Helms, C.W., & Helms, D.R. (1992, June). Multimedia in Education (Report No. IR-016-090). Proceedings of the 25th Summer Conference of the Association of Small Computer Users in Education. North Myrtle Beach, SC. (ERIC Document Reproduction Service No. ED 357 732)

This article discusses the need for multimedia in education and explains how and why the College of Sciences of Clemson University is encouraging the use of multimedia in the science classroom. The university is making technology available by developing and marketing science software suitable for educational use. The use of multimedia is encouraged because 1) it has the ability to reach students through sight, sound and touch, 2) all learning styles can be accommodated, 3) cooperative learning and communication are fostered, and 4) an active learning environment is created.

Smith, M.K., & Wilson, C. (1993, March). Integration of student learning strategies via technology (Report No. IR-016-035). Proceedings of the Fourth Annual Conference on Technology and Teacher Education. San Diego, CA (ERIC Document Reproduction Service No. ED 355 937)

This article examines the link between needed reform in education and advances in technology. The three categories of reform are: changing what is being learned, with a focus on higher-order thinking skills; changing students from passive to active learners; and assessment, moving away from multiple choice examinations to more meaningful evaluation of what students are learning. Four types of instructional strategies are outlined which when incorporated into the curriculum will address the categories of concern. The four are: Tutorial; Exploratory/Problem Solving; Communications; and Tool/Techniques.

O'Connor, J.E. (1993, April). Evaluating the effects of collaborative efforts to improve mathematics and science curricula (Report No. TM-019-862). Paper presented at the Annual Meeting of the American Educational Research Association, Atlanta, GA. (ERIC Document Reproduction Service No. ED 357 083)

This article reports on the results of the ongoing Mathematics and Science Partnership Project (MSPP), designed "to impact mathematics and science curricula through the implementation of innovative technology. Thirteen teachers at six high schools have been provided multimedia workstations, software, and training in implementing the technology. Some results of this effort are presented following the first 2.5 years. Various evaluation methods have been used, including teacher journals, classroom observations, videotaping questionnaires, student interviews, and a quasi-experimental comparison (not yet complete) of a group of students using the technology with a group without access to the technology. Results show teachers are using a more student-centered approach, and using more cooperative learning groups. Student motivation is improved, and students are enthusiastic about technology."

Sherwood, R.D., & Others (1990, April). An evaluative study of level one videodisc based chemistry program (Report No. SE-051-513). Paper presented at a Poster Session at the 63rd. Annual Meeting of the National Association for Research in Science Teaching, Atlanta, GA. (ERIC Document Reproduction Service No. ED 320 772)

"This study evaluated the effectiveness of the use of videodisc technology in a school system. The videodisc 'Understanding Chemistry and Energy '(Systems Impact, 1987) having 20 lessons was used in Physical Science classes (grade 9) and Biology classes (grade 10 and 11) in an experimental school. It was designed to be used with a variety of classes especially classes for studying some aspects of chemistry." A control group in the same school system received traditional instruction. Results on the post-test suggested that use of the videodisc could substantially improve student knowledge.

F. CURRENT INDEX TO JOURNALS IN EDUCATION

Reeves, T.C. (1992) Evaluating interactive multimedia. Educational Technology, 32 (5), 47-52.

This article defines interactive multimedia (IMM) to be a computerized database that allows users to access information in multiple forms including text, graphics, video and audio. The stated goal of using IMM is the improvement of the conditions of teaching and learning in schools. Guidelines and strategies for the evaluation of IMM are discussed. Formative evaluation and formative experimentation are described and goals are selected as a component of the formative experimentation. These goals are focused on 'actualizing' three primary principles of contemporary cognitive learning theory. The three principles mentioned are 1) that learning is a process of knowledge construction, 2) that learning is knowledge dependent, and 3) that learning is highly tuned to the situation in which it takes place. Methods of completing the evaluation are given.

Howson, B. A. & Davis, H. (1992). Enhancing comprehension with videodiscs. Media and Methods, 28 (3), 12-14.

This article discusses the use of videodiscs as away to increase students' comprehension. The benefits of adding visual images to learning activities are described, and videodiscs as sources of data for students to analyze are considered. An example is given of using videodiscs to illustrate concepts in a chemistry lesson.

Smith, E. E., & Westhoff, G. M. (1992). The Taliesin project: Multidisciplinary education and multimedia. Educational Technology, 32 15-23.

"Describes the Taliesin project, a current curriculum materials research and development effort whose main goals are (1) the development of a computer-aided classroom instructional tool for grades six through eight based on hypermedia technology, and (2) the development of a multidisciplinary curriculum to help develop stronger interests in mathematics and science." Hypermedia's structure, which offers information in 'chunks' and has links between the 'chunks', is highly suitable for use with a multidisciplinary curriculum. Training will be provided for teachers in the use of hypermedia.

## G. REVIEW OF EDUCATIONAL RESEARCH

Kozma, R .B. (1991). Learning with Media. Review of Educational Research, 61 179-211.

"This article describes learning with media as a complementary process within which representations are constructed and procedures performed, sometimes by the learner and sometimes by the medium. It reviews research on learning with books, television, computers, and multimedia environments. These media are distinguished by cognitively relevant characteristics of their technologies, symbol systems, and processing capabilities. Studies are examined that illustrate how these characteristics, and the instructional designs that employ them, interact with learner and task characteristics to influence the structure of mental representations and cognitive processes. Of special interest is the effect of media characteristics on the structure, formation and modification of mental models. Implications for research and practice are discussed."

# PART TWO

## RESEARCH PROBLEMS

### Task 2 Examples

**Task 2**

Write an introduction for a research plan. This will include a statement of the specific problem to be investigated in the study, a statement concerning the significance of the problem, a review of related literature, and a testable hypothesis. Include definitions of terms where appropriate.

Since in succeeding Parts you will be performing Tasks as they relate to your problem, you should give careful thought to the selection of a problem. Also, since the research competencies required for the conducting of an experimental study include many of the competencies required for conducting studies representing the other methods of research, and more, it is to your advantage to select a problem which can be investigated experimentally; you will acquire experience with a wider range of competencies and should be able to generalize many of those competencies as they apply to the other methods of research.

Task 2 involves the writing of an introduction to a research plan which follows the guidelines described in Part Two. Following this discussion, examples are presented which illustrate the format and content of such an introduction. These examples, with few modifications, represent Tasks submitted by former students in an introductory research course. Examples from published research could have been used, but these examples more accurately reflect the performance which is expected of you at your current level of research expertise.

More examples are presented for this Task than for succeeding Tasks because students typically have more trouble with Task 2. After years of writing term papers, it is somewhat difficult to get the "hang" of writing a research paper, which requires much more synthesis. The examples presented represent very diverse topics; the hope is that you, depending upon your major field of study, will be able to especially relate to one of them.

**IMPORTANT * IMPORTANT * IMPORTANT * IMPORTANT * IMPORTANT * IMPORTANT**

The Task 2 examples presented do not follow two APA guidelines; they are single-spaced, not double-spaced, and margins are not 1 in. The purpose of these deviations was to save space, i.e., reduce the number of pages in the Student Guide, in order to keep it as affordable as possible for students.

Effect of Portfolio Assessment on the
Writing Achievement of Fourth-Grade Students[1]

Introduction

Standardized testing has been for the past 50 years or so the primary source of information on how well schools have been educating our youth. But over the years, there has been increased criticism concerning the validity of such tests. Too often these tests have been misused rather than properly used for such purposes as accountability and high-stakes decisions.

Many argue that these tests give false information about the status of learning in schools, are biased against certain types of students, focus on the simpler skills that are easily tested - at the expense of higher-order and creative skills, and reduce the teacher to the menial task of "teaching to the teat" (Hambleton & Murphy, 1992; Kennedy, 1992; Popham, 1993; Worthen, 1993). Such commentary has opened the door to alternative forms of assessment.

Authentic assessment is a form of alternative assessment which centers on the direct examination of a student's performance on high-order thinking skills and on significant tasks that are applicable to real-life situations (Kennedy; 1992; Winograd & Jones, 1992; Worthen, 1993). This can be accomplished by implementing a variety of methods, such as, the portfolio (Feur & Fulton, 1993).

According to Chapman (1990), the portfolio is rapidly becoming the most popular used method of assessing writing, offering excellent criteria for teaching and evaluation. Not all educators and experts agree, however. Hambleton and Murphy (1992) for instance, question the validity and reliability of authentic assessment while stressing that research on new forms of assessment are necessary.

Statement of the Problem

The purpose of this study was to investigate the effects of portfolio assessment on the writing achievement of fourth-grade students. Portfolio assessment was defined as a form of authentic assessment in which the student is required to complete a body of writing over a prolonged period of time.

Review of Related Literature

In recent years the processes of writing instruction and learning to write have drastically changed as researchers and teachers concentrate their attention on the steps used by students instead of on the final written product (Farmer, 1986). Entire school systems have been experimenting with the use of portfolios for writing assessment. The Vermont Portfolio Project (Abruscato, 1993) and the Illinois Writing Program (Chapman, 1990) are two examples of continuing research that support this idea. Both approaches are very similar in structure and assessment criteria, and reports for both efforts indicate promising results in terms of writing performance. These results are supported by other efforts. Marchensi (1992), for instance, found that involvement in a portfolio practicum at the middle school level increased both student participation in writing and attitudes toward the writing process.

Although validity and reliability continue to be a problem, the approach shows promise. Farmer (1986), for example, compared process (portfolio) and traditional approaches to large-scale writing assessment and investigated the magnitude, reliability and validity of scores. Results indicated that the quality of writing was high for both groups but considerably higher for the portfolio group. Interrater reliability was moderate regardless of assessment method but significantly lower for the portfolio group, and concurrent validity was low for both methods but not significantly different between methods.

Statement of the Hypothesis

Although there has been some controversy concerning the use of portfolio assessment as a valid, reliable method for assessing a student's performance in writing, the literature suggests that use of this form of assessment is effective. Therefore, it was hypothesized that fourth-grade students who participate in a portfolio assessment program exhibit better performance in writing than those fourth-grade students who participate in a traditional assessment program.

---

[1]Based on a paper by L. E. Marazita, Florida International University, Miami, 1994.

## References


Abruscato, J. (1993). Early results and tentative implications from the Vermont portfolio project. Phi Delta Kappan, 74, 474-477.

Chapman, C. (1990). Authentic Writing Assessment. (Report No. TM-016-137). Washington, DC: American Institutes for Research. (ERIC Document Reproduction Service No. ED 328 606)

Farmer, M. (1986). A comparison of process and traditional approaches to large-scale writing assessment: Investigating score magnitude, interrater reliability, and concurrent validity. Dissertation Abstracts International,47, 158A. (University Microfilms No. DA8605264)

Feur, M. J. , & Fulton, K. (1993). The many faces of performance assessment. Phi Delta Kappan, 74, 478.

Hambleton, R. K., & Murphy, E. (1992). A psychometric perspective on authentic measurement. Applied Measurement in Education, 5, 1-16.

Kennedy, R. (1992). What is performance assessment? New Directions for Education Reform, 1, 21-27.

Marchensi, R. J. (1992). Using Portfolios for More Authentic Assessment of Writing Ability. (Report No. CS-213-456). Practicum paper, Nova University. (ERIC Document Reproduction Service No. ED 347 555)

Polloway, E. A. (1985). Review of Test of Written Language. The ninth mental measurements yearbook (pp. 1600-1602). Highland Park, NJ: Gryphon.

Popham, J. W. (1993). Educational testing in America: What's right, what's wrong? A criterion-referenced perspective. Educational Measurement: Issues and Practice, 12, 11-14.

Winograd, P., & Jones, D. L. (1992). The use of portfolios in performance assessment. New Directions for Education Reform, 1, 37-50.

Worthen, B. R. (1993). Critical issues that will determine the future of alternative assessment. Phi Delta Kappan, 74, 444-454.

## Effect of Peer Tutoring on the Reading Comprehension of Failing Seventh-Grade English Students[2]

### Introduction

There is growing concern about the educational system. Americans increasingly hear about students who have gone through the educational system and are still unable to read. According to Reissman (1989), the last decade has seen little significant improvement in the learning of children or the dropout rate.

Concern about student achievement has led to research in the area of alternative teaching/learning strategies. One such strategy is peer tutoring. Peer tutoring utilizes a major, yet previously unused, resource in schools, children, and greatly expands the schools' teaching capability. With peer tutoring programs, students become more active, more interdependent, and develop more of a feeling of community (Reissman, 1989).

Benefits have been found for teachers, tutors, tutees, and the social climate of the school when peer tutoring is implemented (Hedin, 1987). Students are able to receive the help they need on a one-to-one basis, which is virtually impossible for teachers to accomplish alone. Therefore, teachers are more satisfied when they see their students receiving needed help. Research has shown that there are academic gains for both tutors and tutees involved in peer tutoring programs (Topping, 1989). The social climate of the school improves because students who were once doing poorly in school demonstrate more motivation and enthusiasm for school after peer tutoring (Dombey, 1988).

#### Statement of the Problem

The purpose of this study was to investigate the effect of peer tutoring on the reading comprehension of failing seventh-grade English students. Peer tutoring was defined as a tutorial relationship maintaining an age difference from 1 month to 2 years. Tutor refers to the helping student, and tutee refers to the student receiving help.

#### Review of Related Literature

A question that is often raised concerning the effectiveness of peer tutoring is whether students have the knowledge and ability to work in an instructional capacity. Several research studies have shown that students do have the skill to teach in the manner they were trained (Hawes, 1988; McTeer, 1983; Turnbull & Bronicki, 1989). In the Palincsar, Brown, and Martin (1987) study, seventh-grade reading tutors were taught to use a dialogue procedure involving four comprehension monitoring strategies with their tutees. Although the dialogue procedure was complicated, the tutors successfully modeled the procedure.

Besides questioning peer tutors' teaching ability, some apprehension about implementing peer tutoring programs is based on the fear that peer tutors have nothing to gain in the process. To the contrary, Berliner (1989) found that most students who take a teaching role learn more than they do when they receive instruction or work independently. Peer tutors have benefits other than their own academic learning to be gained. Tutors also learn to be responsible, gain respect from tutees, and are able to study material below their grade level without embarrassment if they are older, lower-ability tutors (Hedin, 1987).

There are several benefits also for tutees. Tutees are able to receive one-to-one, individualized instruction. Some tutees benefit more by learning with a peer, since peers often establish a more similar climate and vocabulary than do students and teachers (Hedin, 1987; Judy, Alexander, Kulikowich, & Willson, 1988; Topping, 1989). There are also gains in self-concept (Hansen, 1986; Topping, 1989) and motivation (Dombey, 1988).

Considering the current status of drop-outs and illiteracy, a more important benefit to tutees may be the improved academic performance resulting from peer tutoring. Peer tutoring has been shown to increase math achievement in elementary students (Pflug, 1987; Greenfield & McNeil, 1987). It has also been shown that substantial gains can be made in vocabulary performance (Hansen, 1986). More importantly, peer tutoring, with respect to reading at the elementary level, has been found to be effective for nonremedial sixth-grade students (Judy, Alexander, Kulikowich, & Wilson, 1988) and for remedial fourth-grade students (Mooney, 1986).

---

[2]Based on a paper by C.D. Collins, Florida International University, Miami, 1991.

Statement of the Hypothesis

Although most of the research on peer tutoring has focused on elementary students, it has shown that peer tutoring is effective in promoting the academic performance of both nonremedial and remedial students. Therefore, it was hypothesized that failing seventh-grade English students who participate in a peer tutoring program have higher reading comprehension scores than failing seventh-grade English students who do not participate in a peer tutoring program.

References

Berliner, D. (1989). Being the teacher helps students learn. Instructor, 98, 12-13.

Dombey, K. W. (1988). Cross-age tutoring works wonders. American Libraries, 19, 726-727.

Greenfield, S. D., & McNeil, M. E. (1987). Improving math performance through a peer tutoring program. (Report No. SE 048 573). (ERIC Document Reproduction Service No. ED 286 735)

Hansen, G. (1986). Cooperative vs. individual learning effects on vocabulary retention. (Report No. CS 008 444). Master's thesis, Kean College of New Jersey. (ERIC Document Reproduction Service No. ED 269 742)

Hawes, H. (1988). Child-to-child: Another path to learning. (Report No. SP 030 536). Hamburg, West Germany: United Nations Educational, Scientific, and Cultural Organization. (ERIC Document Reproduction Service No. ED 300 345)

Hedin, D. (1987). Students as teachers: A tool for improving school climate and productivity. Social Policy, 17, 42-47.

Judy, J. E., Alexander, P. A., Kulikowich, J. M., & Willson, V. L. (1988). Effects of two instructional approaches and peer tutoring on gifted and nongifted sixth-grader students' analogy performance. Reading Research Quarterly, 23, 236-256.

McTeer, J. H. (1983). Peer tutoring as an instructional methodology for social studies teaching. (Report No. SO 014 737). (ERIC Document Reproduction Service No. ED 230 477)

Mooney, C. (1986). The effects of peer tutoring on student achievement. (Report No. CS 008 474). Master's thesis, Kean College of New Jersey. (ERIC Document Reproduction Service No. ED 270 730)

Palincsar, A. S., Brown, A. L., & Martin, S. M. (1987). Peer interaction in reading comprehension. Educational Psychologist, 22, 231-253.

Pflug, E. A. (1987). A comparison of the effect of computer-assisted-instruction and same-age peer-tutoring on math achievement of fourth grade students. Dissertation Abstracts International, 48, 1113A. (University Microfilms No. DA8717040)

Riessman, F. (1989). A school-change paradigm. Education Digest, 54, 10-12.

Topping, K. (1989). Peer tutoring and paired reading: Combining two powerful techniques. The Reading Teacher, 42, 488-494.

Turnbull, K., & Bronicki, G. J. (1989). Children can teach other children. Teaching Exceptional Children, 21, 64-65.

Effect of Conflict Resolution Training on the Number of Student Referrals for Third-Grade Inner-City Students[3]

## Introduction

With an increase in violence across the nation, discipline and school safety have become pressing issues in education. Demographic and socioeconomic shifts in our nation's population and changes in the family structures have placed increasing demands on educators today. The growing level of violence displayed by youth is disrupting schools' abilities to function. Besides providing students with academic development, schools have become more responsible for the socialization and acculturation of out nation's children (Van Acker, 1993).

A variety of crisis management and response strategies have been implemented to promote campus safety and a positive school climate. Traditional discipline procedures, such as detention, expulsion, suspension, and placement in alternative educational programs, merely mete out punishment and are not enough. With the escalation of violence in schools, educators must begin to address these issues proactively. They need to challenge the violence in children's social lives by intervening early and teaching skills to help them learn a broader repertoire for resolving conflicts (Carlson-Paige & Levin, 1993). It is important that conflicts be defined as win/win propositions with both individuals having equal status in the resolution process (Lane & McWhirter, 1992; Sorenson, 1992). To reduce the future probability of undesired behavior, students must be taught the skills needed to behave in the desired fashion.

Children need to learn at a very young age that their problems have two sides. Educators must strive to help children develop an internal locus of control, to counter tension, animosity and aggression. Children need to feel empowered and know that they are capable of creating more positive social relationships without adult intervention. The earlier children are taught these conflict resolution strategies, the better.

### Statement of the Problem

The purpose of this study was to assess whether training in conflict resolution would be effective in reducing the number of student referrals for third-grade inner-city students. Conflict resolution was defined as a form of mediation used in the resolution of disputes. The key elements of conflict resolution are: defining the problem, brainstorming solutions, using negotiation skills, and choosing solutions that satisfy both sides (Carlson-Paige & Levin, 1993).

### Review of Related Literature

All students need to be trained in how to manage conflicts constructively. When students are taught how to negotiate and are given opportunities to mediate their classmates' conflicts, they are given procedures and components to (1) regulate their behavior through self-monitoring, (2) judge what is appropriate given the situation and the perspective of the other person, and (3) modify how they behave accordingly (Johnson, Johnson, Dudley & Burnett, 1992). Conflict resolution is something that can be learned and used in all aspects of life, including school (Glass, 1994).

Several studies show that training in conflict resolution has a positive effect on the social behavior of students (Inkram, 1992; Miller, 1993; Robertson, 1991; Zhang, 1992). After implementation of a conflict resolution program in a middle school in Beltsville, Md., Miller (1993), for example, found that the number of suspensions decreased, school climate improved, the number of student arguments decreased, and student relationships improved.

### Statement of the Hypothesis

While little has been done at the elementary level, research findings suggest that training in conflict resolution has a positive effect on social behavior. Therefore, it was hypothesized that third-grade inner-city students who receive training in conflict resolution have fewer number of student referrals than third-grade inner-city students who do not receive training in conflict resolution.

---

[3]Based on a paper by C. Johnson, Florida International University, Miami, 1994.

References

Carlson-Paige, N. & Levin, D. E. (1993). A constructivist approach to conflict resolution. Education Digest, 58, 10-15.

Glass, R. S. (1994). Keeping the peace. American Teacher, 78, 6-7, 15.

Inkram, M. (1992). The impact of a peer-based student conflict management training program in a middle school. Dissertation Abstracts International, 53, 11A. (University Microfilms No. A19300453)

Johnson, D. W., Johnson, R. T., Dudley, B. & Burnett, R. (1992). Teaching students to be peer mediators. Educational Leadership, 50, 10-13.

Lane, P. S., & McWhirter, J. J. (1992). A peer mediation model: Conflict resolution for elementary and middle school children. Guidance Counselor, 27, 15-23.

Miller, R. W. (1993). In search of peace: Peer conflict resolution. Schools in the Middle, 2, 11-13.

Robertson, G. (1991). School-based peer mediation programs: A natural extension of developmental guidance programs. (Report No. CG-024-334). Information Analysis. (ERIC Document Reproduction Service No. ED 346 425)

Sorenson, D. L. (1992). Conflict resolution and mediation for peer helpers. (Report No CG-024-342). Minneapolis: Educational Media Corporation. (ERIC Document Reproduction Service No. ED 347 414)

Van Acker, R. (1993). Dealing with conflict and aggression in the classroom: What skills do teachers need? Teacher Education and Special Education,16, 23-33.

Zhang, Q. (1992). Social psychological consequences of interpersonal relations: A confirmatory approach to testing Deutch's theory of cooperation and conflict resolution. (Report No. UD-028-809). New York: Columbia University Teachers College. (ERIC Document Reproduction Service No. ED 359 274)

## Effects of Visual Referents on Fifth-Grade Students' Concept Application in Representational Drawing[4]

### Introduction

Over the past decade, much attention has been focused on the need to make art education a more substantive component of general education. An approach called "discipline-based art education" (DBAE) has been promoted as a vehicle for combining four art disciplines: production, history, criticism, and aesthetics. An important aspect of DBAE involves teaching art concepts, i.e., ideas which can be applied to visual constructs. These include art elements (e.g., line, shape) and art principles (e.g., contrast, proportion). In art production there has been a move away from "self-expression" toward "artistic expression" in which concepts are learned and then applied in expressive works.

With the revision of general goals in art education has come discussion regarding methods of implementation. In the teaching of representational drawing, the historical debate has reemerged as to whether students should be encouraged to work only from "life" or from two-dimensional sources as well. Drawing sources are called referents. Three-dimensional (3-D) referents are objects or events to which signs or symbols refer; two-dimensional (2-D) referents are graphic representations of the objects or events, such as drawings and photographs.

Two-dimensional referents may be useful because they serve as examples of the transfer of visual information from a 3-D source to a 2-D surface and may provide students with strategies for doing so in their drawings. Some educators fear, however, that their use may lead to superficial imitation and a reduction of personal expression. While 2-D referents may be useful in teaching art concepts and developing technical skill, their use in art production classes remains a subject of debate.

#### Statement of the Problem

The purpose of this study was to assess the effectiveness of combining 2-D and 3-D referents (versus using only 3-D referents) in representational drawing instruction, upon fifth-grade students' application of art concepts in drawing.

#### Review of Related Literature

A major problem for art educators has been the view of art classes as largely recreational, with little educational value. Recent emphasis has been placed on providing opportunities to identify and apply principles, investigate objects and concepts, and use visual conceptualizations for communication and development of ideas (Samuels, 1986; Silverman, 1989). One of education's highest goals is to develop the ability to synthesize experience, observation and thought, and it is hoped that through DBAE art production will offer a valuable approach to this endeavor (Spratt, 1987). It is further hoped that creating art will become a problem-solving activity in which artworks will be examples of concepts learned in addition to being expressive efforts (Greer, 1984; Rush, 1987, 1989a, 1989b).

In a study conducted to compile and compare research on teaching methods, it was found that two primary interests were the development of art concepts and drawing skill. It was indicated that art concepts are taught by several methods, but that visual examples exerted the greatest influence. Drawing skill was influenced by methods which required close attention to visual qualities (Kerr, 1985).

Many educators have argued that "copying" from 2-D referents has no place in art education. Others, however, view it as useful if presented as "reconceptualization" of graphic images (versus mechanical duplication). Research has shown that a variety of referents has been employed by both prodigies and "ordinary" school children (Duncum, 1984, 1988). Research has also shown that when students were taught figure drawing from three different referents (live models, photographs, or copies of master drawings) results in terms of technical use of art elements did not differ significantly (Dowell, 1990).

Although art educators agree that drawing from "life" is essential, developing concentration and awareness (Foster, 1988; McMullan, 1989), research has suggested that 2-D referents may also be valuable when used with discretion, and in combination with 3-D referents (Duncum, 1988).

---

[4]Based on a paper by L.M. McKinley, Florida International University, Miami, 1990.

Statement of the Hypothesis

While many art educators are opposed to the use of 2-D referents in art education, research has suggested that they may be used effectively, especially in conjunction with 3-D referents. Therefore, it was hypothesized that fifth-grade students who receive representational drawing instruction using both 2-D and 3-D referents demonstrate greater application of art concepts than fifth-grade students who receive representational drawing instruction using 3-D referents only.

## References

Dowell, M. L. (1990). Effects of visual referents upon representational drawing of the human figure. Studies in Art Education, 31, 78-85.

Duncum, P. (1984). How 35 children born between 1724 and 1900 learned to draw. Studies in Art Education, 26, 93-102.

Duncum, P. (1988). To copy or not to copy: A review. Studies in Art Education, 29, 203-210.

Foster, M. (1988). The observation experience. School Arts, 88 (September), 48-49.

Greer, W. D. (1984). Discipline-based art education: Approaching art as a subject of study. Studies in Art Education, 25, 212-218.

Kerr, M. P. (1985). An integrative review of studies on methods of teaching art production in the United States of America (1951-1981). Dissertation Abstracts International, 1814A. (University Microfilms No. DA85-19, 394)

McMullan, J. (1989). Thinking of drawing. Print, (March/April), 53-59.

Rush, J. C. (1987). Evaluating visual concept learning according to within-class similarities among students' art images. Paper presented at the annual meeting of the American Educational Research Association, Washington, DC. (ERIC Document Reproduction Service No. ED 304 364)

Rush, J. C. (1989a). Coaching by conceptual focus: Problems, solutions, and tutored images. Studies in Art Education, 31, 46-57.

Rush, J. C. (1989b). Theory-based teaching: Problem solving in studio art instruction. Paper presented at the annual meeting of the American Educational Research Association, San Francisco. (ERIC Document Reproduction Service No. ED 310 095)

Samuels, A. (1986, November). Toward a revaluing of art education. The Education Digest, 52, 54-57.

Silverman, R. H. (1989, October). Discipline-based art education. The Education Digest, 55, 53-56.

Spratt, F. (1987). Art production in discipline-based art education. Journal of Aesthetic Education, 21, 197-204.

## Effect of Mnemonic Training on the Achievement of High School Geometry Students[5]

### Introduction

The van Hiele model theorizes that students' cognitive development in geometry progresses through a five-step evolution. At the lowest level, students can recognize figures by appearance but cannot perceive their properties. At the next level, students can identify figures and know their properties but cannot readily connect the two. At the highest van Hiele level, students understand the process of formal deduction. A student at this level can understand the role and necessity for indirect proof and proof by contrapositive (Fuys, Geddes, & Tischler, 1988).

Geometry is a semantically rich and highly structured area of study. Low standardized test results over the last five years of geometry testing in Dade County Public Schools suggest that many students never leave the lower levels of cognitive development. One possible explanation for the low test scores is that students are having difficulty retaining the extensive vocabulary and the elaborately structured facts that are the foundation for the higher levels of cognitive development in geometry. Stone (1989) suggests that the skill of memorization has been on the decline since the invention of written language, printing, and electronic communication media. In order for students to succeed in the study of geometry, memory training is necessary.

#### Statement of the Problem

The purpose of this study was to determine if learning mnemonic (memory) techniques would result in greater student achievement of the prescribed objectives of the high school geometry curriculum.

#### Review of the Literature

The mathematics curriculum (K-12) generally is a progressive and consistent endeavor. The study of mathematics is generally manipulative and procedural. Mathematics is a language of symbols and the use of an English vocabulary is minimal. The one exception to this rule is geometry. Perhaps because of its unique characteristics, the study of geometry has been plagued by an increase in student failures and teacher frustrations (McDonald, 1989a, 1989b). Many changes in the way geometry is taught have taken place. Posamentier (1989) thinks that geometry instruction should center on visual justifications of geometric phenomena, while Simon (1989) argues that geometry instruction should be approached intuitively. Regardless of approach, the fact remains that a primary strategy for the learning and teaching of geometry is memorization. Many geometry teachers feel that memorization of basic facts and semantics is essential in order to explore the various geometric concepts, and that student failures in geometry may suggest that students lack the ability to memorize large amounts of information. Support for this view is provided by research which has reported significant findings relating the important connection between mathematics language facility and achievement in mathematics (Bradley, 1987).

In order for most students to succeed in geometry, it would appear that they require some form of memory training. Although not specifically in the area of geometry, a number of studies have shown that students can be taught to remember information using mnemonic devices. Digby and Lewis (1986), Mastropieri, Emezick and Scruggs (1988), Mastropieri and Scruggs (1989), Powell-Brown (1989), and Rebok and Balcerak (1989) have all reported increased achievement by various groups of students taught mnemonic techniques for recalling information. Williamson (1989) concluded that mnemonic devices not only help students remember information but also allow them to retrieve information more accurately for continued use in cognitive development.

#### Statement of the Hypotheses

Research has shown that there is a definite correlation between mathematics language facility and mathematical achievement. Research has also shown that teaching mnemonic techniques can increase students' retention of information. Therefore, it is hypothesized that high school students enrolled in geometry classes who receive mnemonic training as part of their geometry curriculum will score higher on the Dade County Standardized Geometry Test than students enrolled in geometry classes who do not receive mnemonic training.

---

[5]Based on a paper by P.M. Hirko, Sr., Florida International University, Miami, 1990.

References

Bradley, C. A. (1987). The relationship between mathematics language facility and mathematics achievement among junior high school students. Dissertation Abstracts International, 48, 1684A. (University Microfilms No. DA8721019)

Digby, G., & Lewis, C. (1986). Training children to use mnemonic skills: What causes improvements in memory performance. Paper presented at the annual conference of the Developmental Psychology Section of the British Psychological Society, Exeter, England. (ERIC Document Reproduction Service No. ED 208 568)

Fuys, D., Geddes, D., & Tischler, R. (1988) The van Hiele model of thinking in geometry among adolescents (Monograph). Reston, VA: The National Council of Teachers of Mathematics.

Mastropieri, M. A., Emerick, K., & Scruggs, T. E. (1988). Mnemonic instruction of science concepts. Behavioral Disorders, 14(1), 48-56.

Mastropieri, M. A., & Scruggs, T. E. (1989). Mnemonic social studies instruction: Classroom applications. Remedial and Special Education, 10(3), 40-46.

McDonald, J. L. (1989a). Accuracy and stability of cognitive structures and retention of geometric content. Educational Studies in Mathematics, 20, 425-448.

McDonald, J. L. (1989b). Cognitive development and the structuring of geometric content. Journal for Research in Mathematics Education, 20(1), 76-94.

Posamentier, A. S. (1989). Geometry: A remedy for the malaise of middle school mathematics. Mathematics Teacher, 59, 678-680.

Powell-Brown, D. A. (1989). Effects of mnemonic instruction upon retention of vocabulary with learning-disabled children. Dissertation Abstracts International, 50, 3206A. (University Microfilms No. DA9008122)

Rebok, G. W., & Balcerak, L. J. (1989). Memory self-efficacy and performance differences in young and old adults: The effect of mnemonic training. Developmental Psychology, 25, 714-721.

Simon, M. A. (1989). Intuitive understanding in geometry: The third leg. School Science and Mathematics, 89, 373-380.

Stone, J. (1989). Homer's greatest hit. Discover, 10, 78-80.

Williamson, J. (1989). Vocabulary acquisition: New findings. Paper presented at the annual meeting of the Teachers of English to Speakers of Other Languages, San Antonio. (ERIC Document Reproduction Service No. ED 307 801)

# PART THREE

## RESEARCH PLANS

## Task 3 Examples

**Task 3**

For the hypothesis which you have formulated, develop the remaining components of a research plan for a study which you would conduct in order to test your hypothesis. Include the following:

- Method
  - Subjects
  - Instruments
  - Design
  - Procedure
- Data Analysis
- Time Schedule

Following this discussion, examples are presented which illustrate the performance called for by Task 3. These examples represent tasks submitted by two of the students whose Tasks for Part Two were previously presented; consequently, the research plans match the introductions. Keep in mind that since you do not yet possess the necessary level of expertise, the proposed activities described in your plan (and in the examples presented) do not necessarily represent ideal research procedure. You should also be aware that research plans are usually much more detailed. The examples given, however, do represent what is expected of you at this point.

Effect of Portfolio Assessment on the
Writing Achievement of Fourth-Grade Students

## Method

### Subjects

The subjects for this study will be fourth graders at a private elementary school in Miami, Florida. There will be two groups of 30 students each, representing an experimental group and a control group.

### Instrument

The effectiveness of the two approaches to writing assessment will be determined by the administration of a writing achievement test at the end of the study. If a good published test cannot be found, one will be developed.

### Design

The two groups will be randomly formed and posttested at the end of the study. A pretest will not be necessary because Test of Written English scores will be available to check on initial equality of the groups.

### Procedure

From among the pool of fourth graders, 60 will be selected and randomly assigned to 2 groups of 30 each. For one semester, the two groups will participate in two approaches to writing instruction. The experimental group's instruction will be process oriented and use portfolios, and the control group's instruction will be product oriented. Throughout the duration of the study, both groups will cover the same material, use the same text, and meet for the same amount of time. At the end of the semester, both groups will be administered a writing achievement test.

## Analysis of the Data

The writing achievement scores for the two groups will be compared using a statistic appropriate for comparing the scores of two randomly formed groups.

## Time Schedule

| Procedure | Dates |
|---|---|
| Formation of groups and selection of teachers | 8/15 - 9/1 |
| Implementation of treatment | 9/7 - 12/15 |
| Administration of writing achievement test | 12/16 |
| Analysis of the data | 12/17 - 1/2 |
| Report writing | 10/15 - 1/30 |

Effect of Peer Tutoring on the Reading Comprehension
of Failing Seventh-Grade English Students

## Method

### Subjects

The subjects for this study will be selected from among those in the seventh-grade at a Catholic middle school in Miami, Florida, who are failing English. Fifty students will be selected and placed into 1 of 2 groups.

### Instrument

Subjects will be tested at the beginning of the study and at the end of the study with a standardized test of reading comprehension.

### Design

There will be two randomly formed groups of 25 each. Both groups will be pretested and posttested.

### Procedure

At the end of the first semester, seventh-grade students who are failing English will be identified. Fifty students will be randomly selected and randomly assigned to 1 of 2 classes. Both groups will be pretested to establish initial level of reading comprehension. During the second semester, one class will participate in a peer tutoring program and the other will not. Both classes will be taught the same objectives, by the same teacher, using the same text and materials. At the end of the second semester, both groups will be posttested with the reading comprehension test.

## Data Analysis

The reading comprehension scores of the two groups will be compared using a $t$ test. The score comparison will be made twice, once for pretest scores and once for posttest scores.

## Time Schedule

| Event | Beginning-Ending Date |
|---|---|
| Identification of failing students and group formation | 12/15 - 12/20 |
| Pretesting | 1/3 |
| Implementation of treatment | 1/4 - 6/14 |
| Posttesting | 6/15 |
| Data Analysis | 6/16 - 6/30 |
| Report writing | 2/1 - 7/31 |

# PART FOUR

## SUBJECTS

### Exercises

The Objectives for Part Four involve descriptions of four sampling techniques and procedures for applying each technique. If you are going to be tested on the Objectives, do not memorize definitions. If you understand a concept you should be able to explain it in your own words. If asked to explain random sampling, for example, you do not have to (and should not) quote Part Four by saying "random sampling is the process of selecting a sample in such a way that all individuals in the defined population have an equal and independent chance of being selected for the sample." Instead, you might say "random sampling means that every subject has the same chance of being picked and whether or not one subject gets picked has nothing to do with whether or not any other subject gets picked." Your performance on Objectives 2, 4, 6 and 7 may be evaluated through a testing situation which requires you to apply a given sampling procedure to a given set of circumstances. In order to give you practice in applying each of the techniques, a number of situations follow this discussion. Three examples are given for each of the four sampling techniques. Do the first example for each technique; if your responses match the Suggested Responses you are probably ready for a test and for Task 4. If you do any of the examples incorrectly, study the Suggested Response and then do the second example for that technique. If necessary, repeat the process with the third example.

**Exercise IV-1**

List the procedures for using a table of random numbers to select a sample, given the following situations.

1. There are 150 first graders in the population and you want a random sample of 60 students.

1) ______________________________

______________________________

______________________________

2) ______________________________

______________________________

______________________________

3) ______________________________

______________________________

______________________________

4) ______________________________

______________________________

______________________________

5) ______________________________

______________________________

______________________________

6) ______________________________

______________________________

______________________________

2. There are 220 principals in the school system and you want a random sample of 40 principals.

1) ______________________________

______________________________

______________________________

2) ______________________________

______________________________

______________________________

3) ______________________________

______________________________

______________________________

4) ______________________________

______________________________

______________________________

5) ______________________________

______________________________

______________________________

6) ______________________________

______________________________

______________________________

3. There are 320 students defined as gifted in the school system and you want a random sample of 50 gifted students.

1) ______________________________

______________________________

______________________________

2) ______________________________

______________________________

______________________________

3) ______________________________

______________________________

______________________________

4) ______________________________

______________________________

______________________________

5) ______________________________

______________________________

______________________________

6) ______________________________

______________________________

______________________________

**Exercise IV-2**

List the procedures for selecting a stratified sample, given the following situations:

1. There are 500 12th-grade students in the population, you want a sample of 60 students, and you want to stratify on 3 levels of IQ in order to insure equal representation.

1) ______________________________

______________________________

______________________________

2) ______________________________

______________________________

______________________________

2. There are 95 algebra I students in the population, you want a sample of 30 students, and you want to stratify on sex in order to insure equal representation of males and females.

1) ______________________________

______________________________

______________________________

2) ______________________________

______________________________

______________________________

3. There are 240 principals in the school system, you want a sample of 45 principals, and you want to stratify by level, i.e., elementary versus secondary, in order to insure proportional representation. You know that there are approximately twice as many secondary principals as elementary principals.

1) ______________________________

______________________________

______________________________

2) ______________________________

______________________________

______________________________

**Exercise IV-3**

List the procedures for cluster sampling, given the following situations.

1. There are 80 sixth-grade classrooms in the population, each classroom has an average of 30 students, and you want a sample of 180 students.

1) ______________________________

______________________________

2) ______________________________

______________________________

3) ______________________________

______________________________

2. There are 75 schools in the school system, each school has an average of 50 teachers, and you want a sample of 350 teachers.

1) ______________________________

______________________________

2) ______________________________

______________________________

3) ______________________________

______________________________

3. There are 100 kindergarten classes in the school system, each class has an average of 20 children, and you want a sample of 200 children.

1) ______________________________

______________________________

2) ______________________________

______________________________

3) ______________________________

______________________________

**Exercise IV-4**

List the procedures for selecting a systematic sample, given the following situations.

1. You have a list of 2,000 high school students, and you want a sample of 200 students.

1) ______________________________

______________________________

2) ______________________________

______________________________

3) ______________________________

______________________________

2. You have a directory which lists the names and addresses of 12,000 teachers and you want a sample of 2,500 teachers.

1) ______________________________

______________________________

2) ______________________________

______________________________

3) ______________________________

______________________________

3. You have a list of 1,500 junior high school students, and you want a sample of 100 students.

1) ______________________________

______________________________

2) ______________________________

______________________________

3) ______________________________

______________________________

# PART FOUR

## SUBJECTS

## Task 4 Examples

**Task 4**

**Having selected a problem, and having formulated one or more testable hypotheses or answerable questions, describe a sample appropriate for evaluating your hypotheses or answering your questions. This description will include:**

**a) a definition of the population from which the sample would be drawn;**
**b) the procedural technique for selecting the sample and forming groups;**
**c) sample sizes; and**
**d) possible sources of sampling bias.**

**Task 4 includes descriptions of a population and the procedure for selecting a sample from that population. Following this discussion, examples are presented which illustrate the performance called for by Task 4. Again, these examples represent tasks submitted by the same students whose Tasks 2 and 3 were presented. Consequently, the sampling plans represent refinements of the ones included in Task 3.**

## Effect of Portfolio Assessment on the Writing Achievement of Fourth-Grade Students

The sample for this study will be selected from the total population of fourth-grade students at an upper-middle-class, private elementary school in Miami, Florida. The population is approximately 65% Hispanic, 30% Caucasian non-Hispanic, and 5% African American. The fourth-grade population typically comprises 80 - 100 students. Using a table of random numbers, 60 students will be selected and assigned to 2 groups of 30 each; each group will become a class, as will the remaining, unselected fourth graders.

## Effect of Peer Tutoring on the Reading Comprehension of Failing Seventh-Grade English Students

The sample for this study will be selected from the total population of approximately 60 seventh-grade students with Fs in English at an upper-middle-class, private, Catholic middle school in Miami, Florida. The population is 98% Hispanic and largely of Cuban-American descent. Forty students will be randomly selected (using a table of random numbers) and randomly assigned to 2 groups of 20 each. Each group will become one class, and one class will be randomly designated to receive peer tutoring.

# PART FIVE

## INSTRUMENTS

### Exercises

The Objectives for Part Five involve descriptions of various types of validity and reliability, descriptions of the procedures for determining each, descriptions of types of tests, and procedures for selection and administration of tests. Again, if you are going to be tested on the Objectives, do not try to memorize. Instead, see if you can explain each concept in your own words; if you can, you probably will retain the concepts much better and will be able to explain them in a testing situation. Exercises V-1 and V-2 will assist you in understanding the basic concepts of validity and reliability.

Your performance on Objectives 4 and 6 may be evaluated through a testing situation which requires you to apply a given procedure for establishing validity to a given set of circumstances. In order to give you practice in applying each of the procedures, a number of situations are presented in Exercises V-3 and V-4. Three examples are given for each procedure. Do the first example for each technique; if your responses match the Suggested Responses, you are probably ready for a test. If you do either of the examples incorrectly, study the Suggested Response and then do the second example for that procedure. If necessary, repeat the procedure with the third example.

**Exercise V-1**

Match each statement with the appropriate type of validity by placing the letter corresponding to the type of validity on the blank in front of each statement.

_____ 1. Requires item validity and sampling validity.
_____ 2. Is of prime importance for an aptitude test.
_____ 3. Permits substitution of a shorter test for a longer test.
_____ 4. Is most important for an achievement test.
_____ 5. Would be of concern to a developer of a test of aspirations.

A. content
B. construct
C. concurrent
D. predictive

**Exercise V-2**

Match each statement with the appropriate type of reliability by placing the letter corresponding to the type of reliability on the blank in front of each statement.

_____ 1. Requires a correction formula
_____ 2. Estimates stability of scores over time.
_____ 3. Estimates degree to which two tests measure the same thing.
_____ 4. Determines how all items relate to all other items and to the total test.
_____ 5. When corrected, tends to over-estimate reliability.

A. test-retest
B. equivalent-forms
C. split-half
D. rationale equivalence

**Exercise V-3**

List procedures for determining concurrent validity, given the following situations.

1. You want to determine the concurrent validity of a new IQ test for young children.

1) ______________________________________________

______________________________________________

2) ______________________________________________

______________________________________________

3) ______________________________________________

______________________________________________

4) ______________________________________________

______________________________________________

2. You want to determine the concurrent validity of a new self-concept scale for junior high school students.

1) ______________________________________________

______________________________________________

2) ______________________________________________

______________________________________________

3) ______________________________________________

______________________________________________

4) ______________________________________________

______________________________________________

3. You want to determine the concurrent validity of a new reading comprehension test for high school students.

1) ______________________________

______________________________

2) ______________________________

______________________________

3) ______________________________

______________________________

4) ______________________________

______________________________

**Exercise V-4**

List procedures for determining predictive validity, given the following situations.

1. You want to predict success in graduate school and you want to determine the predictive validity of the GRE.

1) ______________________________

______________________________

2) ______________________________

______________________________

3) ______________________________

______________________________

4) ______________________________

______________________________

2. You want to predict level of achievement in algebra I and you want to determine the predictive validity of an algebra I aptitude test.

1) ________________________________________

2) ________________________________________

3) ________________________________________

4) ________________________________________

3. You want to predict success in nursing school and you want to determine the predictive validity of a nursing aptitude test.

1) ________________________________________

2) ________________________________________

3) ________________________________________

4) ________________________________________

# PART FIVE

## INSTRUMENTS

### Task 5 Example

**Task 5**

Having stated a problem, formulated one or more hypotheses or questions, and described a sample, describe three instruments appropriate for collection of data pertinent to the hypothesis or question. For each instrument selected, the description will include:

a) the name, publisher and cost;
b) a description of the instrument;
c) validity and reliability data;
d) the type of subjects for whom the instrument is appropriate;
e) instrument administration requirements;
f) information regarding scoring and interpretation; and
g) reviewers' overall impressions.

Based on these descriptions, indicate which test is most acceptable for your "study" and why.

Task 5 involves description and comparative analysis of three measuring instruments appropriate for the collection of data pertinent to your hypothesis. Since the task is relatively straightforward, only one example which illustrates the performance called for by Task 5 will be presented.

Test One (from 10th MMY, test #396)

(a) Written Expression Test (WET) - 1978
Johnson, C., & Hubly, S.
Rocky Mountain Education Systems
$34.95 per test including picture stimulus, scoring forms and manual (1986 price data).

(b) The Written Expression Test is an individual or group administered written test with six levels (grades 1-6). All levels yield five scores: productivity, mechanics, handwriting, maturity, and composite.

(c) Interrater reliability ranged from .71 to .99, and content validity is discussed in the technical manual.

(d) The WET is appropriate for grades 1.0 to 6.0.

(e) Administration time is approximately 30 minutes.

(f) No particular training requirements are mentioned. A manual is available but according to one reviewer "the style in which it is written is awkward and there are a number of internal contradictions."

(g) According to the reviewers, the WET needs additional work in order to establish its validity and reliability so that it can measure written expression in an objective manner.

Test Two (from 11th MMY, test #477)

(a) Written Language Assessment (WLA) - 1989
Grill, J. J., & Kirwin, M. M.
Academic Therapy Publications
$58 per complete kit including 25 each of 3 writing record forms, 25 scoring/profile forms, manual, and hand counter; $15 per 25 each of 3 writing record forms; $8 per 25 scoring/profile forms; $20 per manual; $12 per hand counter; $20 per specimen set (1989 price data).

(b) The WLA is an individual or group administered written language test with 10 levels (grades 3-12). All levels yield five scores: general writing ability, productivity, word complexity, readability, and written language quotient.

(c) Internal consistency reliability coefficients are presented for each age level. Median coefficients are: general writing ability (.86), productivity (.81), word complexity (.81), readability (.61), and written language quotient (.90). Three studies of interrater reliability indicate that over 95% of the judgments of 2 ratings of general writing ability are within 1 point of each other. Concurrent validity is based on correlations with the Picture Story Language Test (PSLT). Construct validity data consists of moderate intercorrelations among the WLA subtests and moderate correlations with age of examinee.

(d) The WLA is appropriate for grades 3.0 to 12.

(e) Administration time is approximately 60 minutes.

(f) The test forms and the manual are well designed and easy to use. Technical information is presented in clear language that is understandable to those with limited background in statistics. There are no training requirements mentioned.

(g) Both reviewers agreed that the WLA is a new test that is limited by inadequate normative date and a lack of studies supporting its usefulness in a variety of applications. One reviewer observed that the WLA did represent a welcome effort to move writing evaluation in the direction of direct assessment of product, if not process.

Test Three (from 9th MMY, test #1278)

(a) Test of Written Language (TOWL) - 1978t
Hammill, D. D., & Larson, S. C. .
PRO-ED
$46 per complete kit including 50 test/answer sheets, 50 profiles, and manual in storage box; $18 per 50 test/answer sheets; $12 per 50 profiles; $19 per manual (1984 price data).

(b) The TOWL is a group/individual administered written achievement test with 10 levels ranging from 3rd to 12th grade. Six subtests, vocabulary, thematic maturity, spelling, word usage, style, and handwriting, are used. Scores and norms for each subtest are given.

(c) According to the reviewers, content and criterion validity are good. Content validity is based on the acceptance of the model used for the test and the selection of items, whereas, criterion validity was determined through correlation with Myklebust's (1965) Picture Story Language Test (PSLT), the Test of Adolescent Language (TOAL), the Comprehensive Tests of Basic Skills (CTBS), and the teacher ratings of the TOWL's space story. Concurrent validity is statistically significant for correlations with PSLT. Reliability coefficients are reported for internal consistency (.80), test-retest reliability (.62 to .90), and inter-scorer reliability (.93 for thematic maturity, .98 for vocabulary and .76 for handwriting). Standard error of measurement data are reported for age level 12 based on the same data obtained for test-retest reliability.

(d) The TOWL is appropriate for grades 3.0 to 12.

(e) Administration time is approximately 40 minutes.

(f) Directions for scoring and interpretation are clearly presented in the manual, but the possibilities for confusion in scoring are significant. Trained judgement is mandatory for the results to be used with any degree of confidence. Eight sample scored stories are provided to serve as training for the three subtests that are based on the spontaneous format.

(g) Both reviewers agreed that the test has a sound theoretical basis, and is presented in a clear and careful manner. Although caution is suggested in using scores, the test represents a major new direction in the evaluation of written language.

## Conclusion

Each of the tests chosen for the comparative analysis provided data pertaining to the content validity and reliability of the tests. Based on this information, an educated decision as to which test to use was feasible.

According to the reviewers, the WET does not appear to be "adequate for use as a research or a clinical instrument", therefore, it is not recommended for measuring written language. There are many reasons supporting this decision, among them, that the theoretical foundation of the WET is not explained, the development of the instrument is unreported, and the considerations of psychometric quality are unobserved.

The Written Language Assessment (WLA) was eliminated from the final choice due to the reviewers' report, which stated that the test was "limited by inadequate normative data and a lack of studies supporting its usefulness in a variety of applications." Put more simply, content validity is weak. Another reason for discarding this test was that one of the reviewers alluded to the fact that the WLA represents a move towards direct assessment of a final written product, in contrast to process, which is the sole focus of this study.

The Test of Written Language (TOWL) was chosen primarily for its high reliability coefficients and well documented content validity. Internal consistency reliability of the subtests at different grade levels reached or exceeded .80 and were statistically significant. Test-retest reliability coefficients ranged from .62 to .90 for the 6 subtests, and inter-scorer reliability coefficients ranged from .76 to .98. Although no coefficients are reported for validity, the authors provide an extensive discussion of questions related to the validity of the test. Criterion validity was determined through correlation with previously mentioned tests, such as the PSLT, TOAL and CTBS. Concurrent validity with the PSLT proved to be statistically significant. The TOWL was also chosen on the basis that it was to be administered with the sole purpose of documenting a student's progress in a special writing program; three of the six subtests, handwriting, vocabulary, and thematic maturity, were based on the assessment of a spontaneous writing sample which was considered to be the appropriate vehicle to test these concepts. Finally, the TOWL was chosen because administration time is only 40 minutes, directions for scoring and interpretation are clearly stated in the manual, and sample scored stories are presented for training purposes.

# PART SIX

## RESEARCH METHODS AND PROCEDURES

### Exercises

**Exercise VI-1**

Read each of the statements following the list of threats to validity. For each statement, identify the threat represented and place its letter in the blank in front of each description.

A. history
B. maturation
C. testing
D. instrumentation
E. statistical regression
F. differential selection
G. mortality
H. pretest-treatment interaction
I. selection-treatment interaction
J. reactive arrangement

1. _______ A number of students in the experimental after-school fitness program dropped out when baseball season began.
2. _______ The treatment group behaved very well because the observers were recording their behavior.
3. _______ The first-grade students in the reading program being evaluated were also receiving perceptual-motor training in their physical education classes.
4. _______ The 30 students with the lowest scores on the multiple-choice vocabulary test were selected for participation in a remedial program.
5. _______ The students discussed the questions following administration of the pretest on American literature.

**Exercise VI-2**

Read each of the statements following the list of designs. For each statement, identify the most appropriate design and place its letter on the blank in front of the statement.

A. one-group pretest-posttest
B. static group comparison
C. pretest-posttest control group
D. posttest-only control group
E. nonequivalent control group
F. time series
G. counterbalanced
H. single subject

1. _______ The population is emotionally disturbed children in need of self-control education.
2. _______ Our grant requires that we show that our approach improved the coordination of each participant.
3. _______ Random assignment is possible and we will be measuring computation ability after 9 months of participation in 1 of 2 curricula.
4. _______ Students are already in classes. We will compare the social studies achievement of students in classes using interactive videodiscs with the achievement of students in classes using the usual textbook and materials.
5. _______ We have randomly assigned students to 12 physical education classes - 6 coed classes, 3 all male classes, and 3 all female classes - and we will be measuring feelings concerning coeducational physical education classes.

# PART SIX

## RESEARCH METHODS AND PROCEDURES

### Task 6 Examples

**Task 6**

Having stated a problem, formulated one or more hypotheses, described a sample, and selected one or more measuring instruments, develop the method section of a research report. This should include a description of subjects, instrument(s), research design, and specific procedures.

Task 6 involves development of the method section of your research report. The examples which follow were prepared by the same students who prepared previous examples and you therefore should be able to see how Task 6 builds on previous Tasks. Keep in mind that Tasks 3, 4 and 5 will not appear in your final research report; Task 6 will. Therefore, each of the important points in those previous tasks should be included in Task 6. Since earlier it was recommended that you design an experimental study, the examples represent experimental research. If your study represents one of the other methods of research, you should be able to generalize from the following examples.

Effect of Portfolio Assessment on the
Writing Achievement of Fourth-Grade Students.

Method

Subjects

The sample for this study was selected from the total population of 83 fourth-grade students at an upper-middle-class, private elementary school in Miami, Florida. The population is approximately 65% Hispanic, 30% Caucasian non-Hispanic, and 5% Black American. Using a table of random numbers, 56 students were randomly selected and randomly assigned to 2 groups of 28 each.

Instrument

In this study, the Test of Written Language (TOWL) was used as the measuring instrument. The TOWL was designed for grades 3 - 12 and is suitable for testing both individuals and groups of students. The main purpose of the TOWL is to fill a void in the assessment of written language and its subskills. It consists of six subtests: 1) vocabulary; 2) thematic maturity; 3) spelling; 4) word usage; 5) style (capitalization & punctuation); and 6) handwriting. Three of the six subtests (handwriting, vocabulary, and thematic maturity) are based on the assessment of a spontaneous writing sample. The three subtests not based on the writing sample (spelling, word usage, and style) consist of the typical multiple choice or right/wrong type of item questions common to other written language achievement tests. The findings of a well conducted assessment effort can be used to: 1) identify students who perform significantly more poorly than their peers in written expression and who as a result need special help; 2) determine a student's particular strengths and weaknesses in various writing abilities; 3) document a student's progress in a special writing program; and 4) conduct research in writing. This instrument was administered in one session lasting 40 minutes.

Although no coefficients are reported for validity, the authors provide an extensive discussion of questions related to the validity of the test. According to Polloway (1985, p.1602), "content validity is based on the acceptance of the model used for the test and the subsequent selection of items; rationales are provided for both concerns and no significant problems are noted in this area." Criterion validity was determined through correlation with the Myklebust's (1965) Picture Story Language Test (PSLT), the Test of Adolescent Language (TOAL), the Comprehensive Tests of Basic Skills (CTBS), and the teacher ratings of the TOWL's space story. Concurrent validity data with the PSLT is based on the administration of both instruments to a group of elementary students, and although the resulting correlations are generally statistically significant, the author suggests that they must be viewed cautiously since a number of researchers have questioned the PSLT's validity and reliability. Data on predictive validity are not presented.

Reliability data on the TOWL is presented for internal consistency, test-retest reliability, inter-scorer reliability, and standard error of measurement. Internal consistency reliability of the subtests was determined using the split-half method, corrected with the Spearman-Brown formula. The sample consisted of 432 elementary students at different grade levels, and all coefficients reached or exceeded .80 and were statistically significant. Test-retest reliability data are presented from three studies where students were retested after 2, 3, and 4 weeks respectively; the resulting coefficients ranged from .62 to .90 for the six subtests. The coefficients for inter-scorer reliability were .93 for thematic maturity; .98 for vocabulary; and .76 for handwriting. Standard error of measurement data is reported for age level 12 based on the same data obtained for test-retest reliability.

Direction for the administration and scoring of the TOWL are presented in a clear and concise manner. No significant problems are encountered which might be caused by vague instructions to either examiners or students; and although all users of this instrument will undoubtedly have suggestions for modifying and improving TOWL, Polloway (1985, p. 1602) states that it "offers the most structurally sound and instructionally relevant instrument currently available in the area of written language."

Experimental Design

The design used in this study was the posttest-only control group design (see Figure 1). This design was chosen on the premise that random assignment to group was feasible, and a pretest was not necessary since all students in the study had been previously administered the Test of Written English and scores were available. Choosing this particular design eliminated the majority of threats posed to the internal and external validity of the study. Mortality, a potential threat to internal validity in this design, was not a problem due to the duration of the study (eight weeks) and the consistency of both groups throughout the course of the study.

| Group | Assignment | n | Treatment | Posttest |
|---|---|---|---|---|
| 1 | Random | 28 | Portfolio Assessment Program | TOWL[a] |
| 2 | Random | 28 | Traditional Assessment Program | TOWL |

[a]Test of Written Language

Figure 1. Experimental design.

Procedure

Prior to the beginning of the second marking period for the 1993-1994 school year, 56 of the 83 fourth-grade students were randomly selected and randomly assigned to 2 groups of 28 each. Each group represented a creative writing class which third through sixth graders are requires to take during their second marking period. One of the classes was randomly chosen to participate in the portfolio instruction program. Two of the three creative writing teachers were randomly selected and randomly assigned to one of the classes. Both teachers were female with similar teaching experience, and familiar with authentic assessment approaches.

The study was designed to last eight weeks (one marking period), officially beginning on the first day of the second marking period. The teacher of the control group taught creative writing using the traditional method of instruction. This included lecturing and instruction on the subject matter, and class discussion of students' writing pieces. Her main role was to provide a guide on how to accomplish each of the different writing tasks, such as , how to write a short story, a poem, a letter, and so forth. Each student was graded on the performance of each finished product.

The approach used by the teacher of the experimental group was similar to that of the control group to the extent that she too included lecturing on the subject matter and held class discussions on students' writing pieces. The main difference makes itself evident in the approach or process of how the student accomplished each writing task. For instance, each student kept a portfolio or a history of each writing assignment. This included rough drafts and revisions, with personal feedback from the teacher providing suggestions for improvement before the final work was due. Each student was graded not only on the finished product but on the writing process as well.

Throughout the duration of the study, each class covered the same material, used the same text, and the writing assignments were the same in number and context. Each class met early in the morning for 55 minutes.

In order to compare their writing skills, the TOWL was administered to both classes on the last day of the marking period.

Effect of Peer Tutoring on the Reading Comprehension
of Failing Seventh-Grade English Students

## Method

### Subjects

The sample for this study was selected from the total population of 60 seventh-grade students with Fs in English at an upper-middle-class, private, Catholic middle school in Miami, Florida. The population was 98% Hispanic and largely of Cuban-American descent. Forty students were randomly selected and randomly assigned to 2 groups of 20 each.

### Instrument

The American School Achievement Tests: Reading, Advanced Level (grades 7-9) was the measuring instrument for this study. This test is designed to measure reading comprehension by utilizing two subtests: sentence and word meaning, and paragraph meaning. The authors of the test provide suitable testing and scoring information with low performance students in mind. The content validity is described as good and a thorough discussion of content describes that it was based on several children's textbooks and the judgment of experts. Concurrent validity is excellent with several major achievement batteries (California Achievement Test, Metropolitan Achievement Test, and Stanford Achievement Test), ranging from .88 to .93. The reliability is also quite good (.89-.94). A reviewer supports use of the instrument by stating that it is solid and well-developed (Fry, 1979).

### Experimental Design

The design used in this study was the posttest-only control group design (see Figure 1). This design was chosen because it controls for many sources of invalidity and because random assignment to groups was feasible. A pretest was not necessary since all students in the study were assumed to have roughly equal knowledge of the dependent variable, and Stanford Achievement Test scores from annual spring testing were available to check initial group equivalence. Mortality, a potential threat to this design, was not a problem since the study lasted only 6 weeks and the group sizes remained constant.

| Group | Assignment | n | Treatment | Posttest |
|---|---|---|---|---|
| 1 | Random | 20 | Peer Tutoring Plus Regular Instructional Program | ASA:R[a] |
| 2 | Random | 20 | Regular Instructional Program | ASA:R |

[a] American School Achievement Test: Reading

Figure 1. Experimental design.

### Procedure

Prior to the beginning of the 1990-1991 school year, 40 of the 60 seventh-grade students who had received an F in English the previous year were randomly selected and randomly assigned to 2 groups of 20. By a coin toss, one group was randomly chosen to participate in peer tutoring. The control group would have regular English instruction only. All 142 seventh-grade English students, including the 40 in the study, were then randomly assigned to four English classes. One class had 4 experimental and 5 control students; a second class had 6 and 6; a third, 5 and 5, and a fourth, 5 and 4.

The 20 experimental students were randomly assigned a peer tutor. Peer tutors were all eighth-grade members of the National Junior Honor Society with cumulative grade point averages from 3.5 to 4.00. The peer tutors were trained to ask tutees recall and interpretation questions about reading material and were also trained to help tutees recall and apply the use of vocabulary definitions. The tutor/tutee pairs met 4 days a week, after school, for 45 minutes per day, for 6 weeks. Mondays and Wednesdays the pairs worked on regular instruction reading material and Tuesdays and Thursdays the pairs worked on regular instruction vocabulary material. The control group received regular classroom instruction only for 6 weeks.

All students in the experimental and control groups had the same English teacher for regular classroom instruction. All classes were taught the same material, from the same textbook, on the same day. After the 6th week of peer tutoring, the American School Achievement Test: Reading was administered to all English students during their English class.

# PART SEVEN

## DATA ANALYSIS AND INTERPRETATION

### Exercises

Exercise VII-1 assesses your ability to select the appropriate statistic for a given research situation. Exercise VII-2 assesses your ability to calculate the various statistics demonstrated in Part VII of the text. The suggested responses for this exercise show the steps involved in arriving at the final answer. Corresponding STATPAK printouts are also given for those of who will be using the software that accompanies the text. Following Exercise VII-2, instructions for using STATPAK are presented. Use this exercise to check your ability to use STATPAK as well as your ability to correctly compute the statistics.

**Exercise VII-1**

Read each of the descriptions following the list of inferential statistics. For each description, identify the appropriate statistic and place its letter on the blank in front of the description.

A. $\underline{t}$ test for independent samples

B. $\underline{t}$ test for nonindependent samples

C. simple analysis of variance

D. Scheffe test

E. factorial analysis of variance

F. analysis of covariance

G. chi square

1. _______ Four randomly formed groups of $\underline{n}$ = 20 each were administered a standardized reading achievement test as a posttest and $\underline{F}$ = 7.42. You want to know if the performance of the three experimental groups is significantly greater than the performance of the control group.

2. _______ From a pool of 115 seventh-grade students identified as potential drop-outs, you are going to form two matched groups of $\underline{n}$ = 25. Matching will be based on self-esteem scores. Students in one group will each be assigned a ninth-grade mentor; students in the other group will not. At the end of the study you are going to compare the attendance of the two groups.

3. _______ Two randomly formed groups, one experimental and one control, have been administered a pretest to measure comprehension of scientific principles. You want to statistically compare the posttest scores and we want to use the pretest scores to increase the power of the statistical test.

4. _______ A group of randomly selected high school teachers ($\underline{n}$ = 100), middle school teachers ($\underline{n}$ = 100), and elementary school teachers ($\underline{n}$ = 100) were asked the following question: "Would you recommend a career in teaching to your students?"

5. _______ Two randomly formed groups will be asked to read a number of passages. One group will be taught strategies for remembering facts and concepts, the other will not. At the end of the study both groups will be tested on the reading passages and the retention level of the groups will be compared.

**Exercise VII-2**

The purpose of this exercise is to give you practice in calculating the various statistics. Perform the required operations yourself before checking the Suggested Responses. Double check all your figures. Students rarely have trouble with the statistical formulas; it is usually the arithmetic that hangs them up.

| X |
|---|
| 2 |
| 4 |
| 4 |
| 5 |
| 6 |
| 6 |
| 6 |
| 7 |
| 8 |
| 9 |

---

$\bar{X}$ =

SD =

$Z_1$ =

$Z_2$ =

$Z_3$ =

$Z_4$ =

$Z_5$ =

$Z_6$ =

$Z_7$ =

$Z_8$ =

$Z_9$ =

$Z_{10}$ =

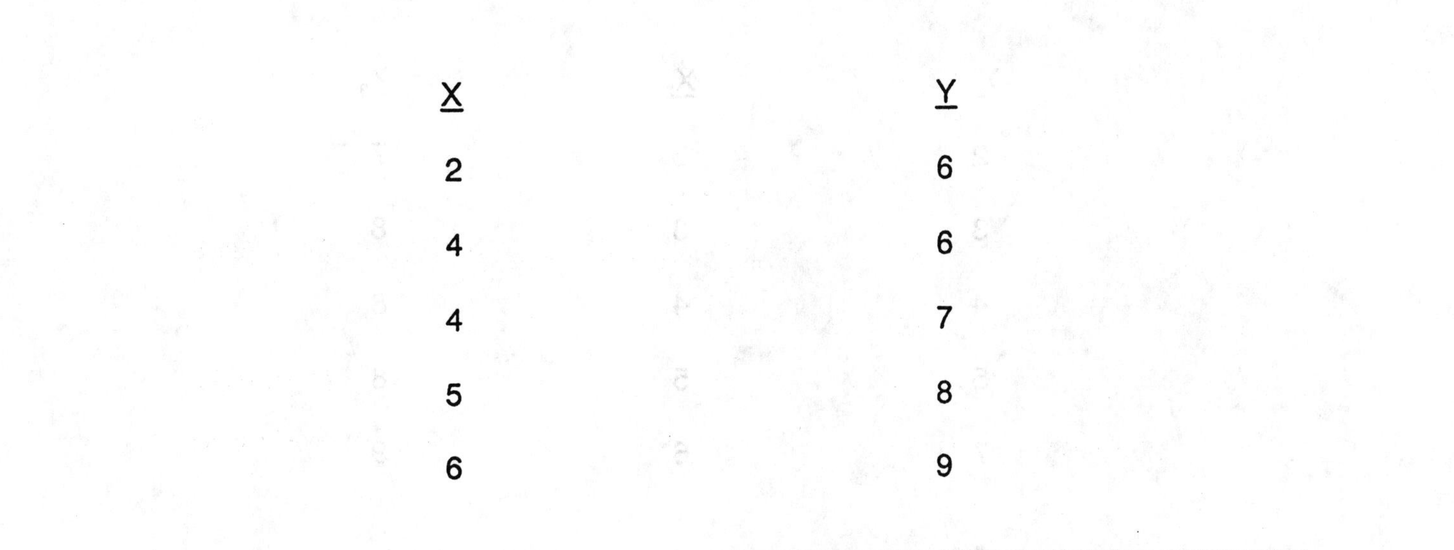

| X | Y |
| --- | --- |
| 2 | 6 |
| 4 | 6 |
| 4 | 7 |
| 5 | 8 |
| 6 | 9 |

$r$ =

| $\underline{X_1}$ | $\underline{X_2}$ | $\underline{X_3}$ |
|---|---|---|
| 2 | 3 | 7 |
| 3 | 3 | 8 |
| 4 | 4 | 8 |
| 5 | 5 | 8 |
| 7 | 6 | 9 |

---

$\underline{t}$ test for independent samples ($\alpha$ = .05)
for the $X_1$ and $X_2$ scores

WORK SPACE

$\underline{t}$ test for nonindependent samples ($\alpha = .05$) for the $X_2$ and $X_3$ scores

Simple analysis of variance for 3 groups ($\alpha = .05$)
for the $X_1$, $X_2$, and $X_3$ scores

WORK SPACE

The Scheffé test ($\alpha$ = .05)

for the $\overline{X}_1$, versus $\overline{X}_2$, $\overline{X}_2$ versus $\overline{X}_3$.

and $\overline{X}_1$ versus $\overline{X}_3$ comparisons

Chi Square - - $\chi^2$ ($\alpha = .05$)
for the $X_1$, $X_2$, and $X_3$ sums

## How to Use STATPAK

STATPAK is available in two versions, one for use with Macintosh micros and one for use with MS DOS (IBM compatible) computers. Your instructor will give you the disk that is appropriate for the hardware available to you.

The steps involved in using STATPAK with a Macintosh computer are as follows:

1. Insert the disk (with the appropriate side up) into Drive 1 and close the disk drive door.
2. Turn on the monitor (if necessary).
3. Turn on the computer.
4. Turn on the printer (if you have one and wish to make hardcopies).
5. The computer will "boot up" and load the program. When the program has been loaded, follow the directions printed on the screen.

The steps involved in using STATPAK with an MS DOS computer are as follows:

1. Insert the system disk which came with your computer into Drive A.
2. Turn on the monitor (if necessary).
3. Turn on the computer.
4. Turn on printer (if you have one and wish to make hardcopies).
5. The computer will "boot up" and may ask you for the date and the time. Respond by simply pressing the ENTER key until you have the prompt A> on your screen.
6. When you have the prompt A> remove the system disk and insert the STATPAK disk.
7. Type in STATPAK and press the ENTER key.
8. When the program has been loaded, follow the directions printed on the screen.

That's it! STATPAK is so user friendly, you could probably use it without further instruction. Just to be on the safe side, however, a basic overview of the program will be presented. One general procedure to note is that in order to move from screen to screen or to enter a response, you simply press the RETURN or ENTER key. For example, if you select option 3, Pearson $r$, from the menu, simply type 3 and then press RETURN. If you are asked a yes-no question such as "Would you like a hardcopy?" type Y or N and press the RETURN or ENTER key. If you make an inappropriate entry, the program will "trap" it, beep the speaker, and indicate the nature of your error.

STATPAK begins with screens that present information such as the name of the program and its author. Following the introductory information, the menu appears as follows:

Enter the number of your choice:

1. MEAN AND STANDARD DEVIATION
2. SPEARMAN RHO
3. PEARSON $r$
4. z AND T Scores
5. $t$ TEST FOR INDEPENDENT SAMPLES
6. $t$ TEST FOR NONINDEPENDENT SAMPLES
7. ANOVA
8. ONE-DIMENSIONAL CHI SQUARE
9. TWO-DIMENSIONAL CHI SQUARE
10. QUIT

You type the number of your choice and press RETURN. The program verifies your selection so that if you inadvertently type the wrong number, you are given an opportunity to make the correction. "Program Loading" then flashes on the screen, followed by a request for your data. For each statistic, you are given instructions for entering your data, and an opportunity to make corrections (in case you inadvertently enter one or more incorrect scores). Scores are entered one at a time; you type the first score and press RETURN, type the next score and press RETURN, and so on. (When you are asked by the program to put in an item, this means the same as score). When you are through, you type END and press RETURN.

The program then computes the chosen statistic and asks you if you would like a hardcopy, i.e., if you would like the results printed out. You then respond Y (yes) or N (no) and press RETURN. If you enter N, results are displayed on the screen.

---

Note: If you enter Y and nothing happens, make sure the printer is on!

---

You are then asked if you would like to 1) run the same program again, or 2) return to STATPAK. If you chose 2, you go back to the menu. When you are completely finished, you type 10 (quit) and press RETURN. You then remove the disk, turn off the printer, and turn off the computer (turn off the monitor, if necessary).

The displayed or printed results for some of the statistics include one or more steps as well as the final answer. For example, in addition to the standard deviation (SD), you are also given the sum of the squared scores ($EX^2$). For other statistics (i.e. Pearson *r*, *t* test for nonindependent samples, ANOVA), you are simply given the correct answer, *N*, and *df*, and are given the option to check you work, i.e., to see the steps that contributed to the final answer. In both cases, the steps are available to you to assist you in locating errors if your answer is not very close (within rounding differences) of the answer given.

---

Note: E is used to represent the summation sign.
R is used to represent *r*.

---

That's all there is to it. Whether this is your first experience using a micro or just your latest, you will appreciate just how user friendly STATPAK is. As always - trust me!

# PART SEVEN

## DATA ANALYSIS AND INTERPRETATION

### Task 7 Example

**Task 7**

Based on Tasks 2-6, which you have already completed, write the results section of a research report. Specifically:

1. Generate data for each of the subjects in your study.
2. Summarize and describe the data using descriptive statistics.
3. Statistically analyze the data using inferential statistics.
4. Interpret the results in terms of your original research hypothesis.
5. Present the results of your data analysis in a summary table.

Task 7 involves computation and interpretation of the descriptive and inferential statistics which are appropriate given your research hypothesis. The example which follows includes the written portion of Task 7 as well as the related calculations and verifying STATPAK printouts.

Effect of Portfolio Assessment on the
Writing Achievement of Fourth-Grade Students

Results

A $t$ test for independent samples ( $\alpha$ = .05) was used to compare the posttest results of the experimental and control groups. This statistical technique was utilized because it was believed that assumptions required for use of a parametric test were met, e.g., subjects were randomly assigned to groups. It was found that the means of the two groups differed significantly (see table 1). Therefore, the original hypothesis that "fourth-grade students who participate in a portfolio assessment program exhibit better performance in writing than those fourth-grade students who participate in a traditional assessment program" were supported.

Table 1

Posttest Means, Standard Deviations, and $t$ Tests for the Experimental and Control Groups

| | Group | | |
|---|---|---|---|
| | Portfolio assessment[a] | Traditional assessment[a] | $t$ |
| $M$ | 92.54 | 82.18 | 5.23* |
| $SD$ | 5.68 | 8.80 | |

Note. Maximum score = 110

[a] $n$ = 28

*$p$< .05.

| | EXPERIMENTAL | | CONTROL | |
|---|---|---|---|---|
| S | $X_1$ | $X_1^2$ | $X_2$ | $X_2^2$ |
| 1 | 80 | 6400 | 67 | 4489 |
| 2 | 80 | 6400 | 69 | 4761 |
| 3 | 83 | 6889 | 70 | 4900 |
| 4 | 85 | 7225 | 70 | 4900 |
| 5 | 85 | 7225 | 71 | 5041 |
| 6 | 87 | 7569 | 73 | 5329 |
| 7 | 89 | 7921 | 73 | 5329 |
| 8 | 90 | 8100 | 75 | 5625 |
| 9 | 90 | 8100 | 78 | 6084 |
| 10 | 93 | 8649 | 78 | 6084 |
| 11 | 93 | 8649 | 81 | 6561 |
| 12 | 94 | 8836 | 81 | 6561 |
| 13 | 94 | 8836 | 81 | 6561 |
| 14 | 94 | 8836 | 84 | 7056 |
| 15 | 95 | 9025 | 84 | 7056 |
| 16 | 95 | 9025 | 85 | 7225 |
| 17 | 95 | 9025 | 85 | 7225 |
| 18 | 95 | 9025 | 85 | 7225 |
| 19 | 95 | 9025 | 86 | 7396 |
| 20 | 96 | 9216 | 86 | 7396 |
| 21 | 96 | 9216 | 87 | 7569 |
| 22 | 96 | 9216 | 87 | 7569 |
| 23 | 97 | 9409 | 90 | 8100 |
| 24 | 97 | 9409 | 93 | 8649 |
| 25 | 98 | 9604 | 93 | 8649 |
| 26 | 99 | 9801 | 95 | 9025 |
| 27 | 100 | 10000 | 96 | 9216 |
| 28 | 100 | 10000 | 98 | 9604 |
| | $\Sigma X_1 = 2591$ | $\Sigma X_1^2 = 240631$ | $\Sigma X_2 = 2301$ | $\Sigma X_2^2 = 191185$ |

$$\overline{X_1} = \frac{\Sigma X_1}{n_1} = \frac{2591}{28}$$

$$\overline{X_1} = 92.54$$

$$\overline{X_2} = \frac{\Sigma X_2}{n_2} = \frac{2301}{28}$$

$$\overline{X_2} = 82.18$$

$$SD_1 = \sqrt{\frac{SS_1}{n_1 - 1}} \qquad SD_2 = \sqrt{\frac{SS_2}{n_2 - 1}}$$

$$SS_1 = \Sigma x_1^2 - \frac{(\Sigma x_1)^2}{n_1}$$
$$= 240631 - \frac{(2591)^2}{28}$$
$$= 240631 - \frac{6713281}{28}$$
$$= 240631 - 239760.04$$
$$SS_1 = 870.96$$

$$SS_2 = \Sigma x_2^2 - \frac{(\Sigma x_2)^2}{n_2}$$
$$= 191185 - \frac{(2301)^2}{28}$$
$$= 191185 - \frac{5294601}{28}$$
$$= 191185 - 189092.89$$
$$SS_2 = 2092.11$$

$$SD_1 = \sqrt{\frac{870.96}{28-1}} = \sqrt{\frac{870.96}{27}}$$
$$= \sqrt{32.26}$$
$$SD_1 = 5.68$$

$$SD_2 = \sqrt{\frac{2092.11}{28-1}} = \sqrt{\frac{2092.11}{27}}$$
$$= \sqrt{77.49}$$
$$SD_2 = 8.80$$

$$t = \frac{\bar{X}_1 - \bar{X}_2}{\sqrt{\left(\frac{SS_1 + SS_2}{n_1 + n_2 - 2}\right)\left(\frac{1}{n_1} + \frac{1}{n_2}\right)}} = \frac{92.54 - 82.18}{\sqrt{\left(\frac{870.96 + 2092.11}{28 + 28 - 2}\right)\left(\frac{1}{28} + \frac{1}{28}\right)}} = \frac{10.36}{\sqrt{\left(\frac{2963.07}{54}\right)(.036 + .036)}}$$

$$= \frac{10.36}{\sqrt{(54.87)(.072)}} = \frac{10.36}{\sqrt{3.95}} = \frac{10.36}{1.98} = 5.23$$

$t = 5.23 \quad df = 54, \; p < .05.$

Note: The $t$ table does not have $df = 54$. To be conservative I used $df = 60$. For $df = 60$, and $p = .05$, the table value is 2.000.

STANDARD DEVIATION FOR SAMPLES AND POPULATIONS

| STATISTIC | VALUE |
|---|---|
| NO. OF SCORES (N) | 28 |
| SUM OF SCORES ($\Sigma X$) | 2591.00 |
| MEAN ($\overline{X}$) | 92.54 |
| SUM OF SQUARED SCORES ($\Sigma X^2$) | 240631.00 |
| SUM OF SQUARES (SS) | 870.96 |
| STANDARD DEVIATION FOR A POPULATION | 5.58 |
| STANDARD DEVIATION FOR A SAMPLE | 5.68 |

## STANDARD DEVIATION FOR SAMPLES AND POPULATIONS

| STATISTIC | VALUE |
|---|---|
| NO. OF SCORES (N) | 28 |
| SUM OF SCORES ($\Sigma X$) | 2301.00 |
| MEAN ($\overline{X}$) | 82.18 |
| SUM OF SQUARED SCORES ($\Sigma X^2$) | 191185.00 |
| SUM OF SQUARES (SS) | 2092.11 |
| STANDARD DEVIATION FOR A POPULATION | 8.64 |
| STANDARD DEVIATION FOR A SAMPLE | 8.80 |

t-TEST FOR INDEPENDENT SAMPLES

| STATISTIC | VALUE |
|---|---|
| NO. OF SCORES IN GROUP ONE | 28 |
| SUM OF SCORES IN GROUP ONE | 2591.00 |
| MEAN OF GROUP ONE | 92.54 |
| SUM OF SQUARED SCORES IN GROUP ONE | 240631.00 |
| SS OF GROUP ONE | 870.96 |
| NO. OF SCORES IN GROUP TWO | 28 |
| SUM OF SCORES IN GROUP TWO | 2301.00 |
| MEAN OF GROUP TWO | 82.18 |
| SUM OF SQUARED SCORES IN GROUP TWO | 191185.00 |
| SS OF GROUP TWO | 2092.11 |
| t-VALUE | 5.23 |
| DEGREES OF FREEDOM (*df*) | 54 |

# PART EIGHT

## RESEARCH REPORTS

### Task 8 Example

**Task 8**

**Based on Tasks 2, 6, and 7, prepare a research report which follows the general format for a thesis or dissertation.**

**Task 8 entails combining Tasks 2, 6, and 7, preparing preliminary pages (including an abstract), and adding a discussion section. The example which follows represents the synthesis of the previously presented tasks related to the effect of portfolio assessment.**

# Effect of Portfolio Assessment on the Writing Achievement of Fourth-Grade Students

Lucila E. Marazita

Florida International University

Submitted in partial fulfillment of

the requirements for EDF 5481

April, 1994

# Table of Contents



---

[1]Example page numbers are located on the upper-right-hand corner of each page.

## List of Tables and Figures

Abstract

The purpose of this study was to investigate the effect of portfolio assessment on the writing achievement of fourth-grade students. Using a posttest-only control group design and a $t$ test for independent samples, it was found that after approximately 8 weeks the class ($n$ = 28) in the portfolio assessment program scored significantly higher on the Test of Written Language than the class($n$ = 28)in the traditional assessment program[$t(54) = 5.29$, $p < .05$]. It was concluded that the portfolio assessment strategy was effective in promoting an increase in achievement in writing of the participating students.

Introduction

Standardized testing has been for the past 50 years or so the primary source of information on how well schools have been educating our youth. But over the years, there has been increased criticism concerning the validity of such tests. Too often these tests have been misused rather than properly used for such purposes as accountability and high-stakes decisions.

Many argue that these tests give false information about the status of learning in schools, are biased against certain types of students, focus on the simpler skills that are easily tested - at the expense of higher-order and creative skills, and reduce the teacher to the menial task of "teaching to the teat" (Hambleton & Murphy, 1992; Kennedy, 1992; Popham, 1993; Worthen, 1993). Such commentary has opened the door to alternative forms of assessment.

Authentic assessment is a form of alternative assessment which centers on the direct examination of a student's performance on high-order thinking skills and on significant tasks that are applicable to real-life situations (Kennedy; 1992; Winograd & Jones, 1992; Worthen, 1993). This can be accomplished by implementing a variety of methods, such as, the portfolio (Feur & Fulton, 1993).

According to Chapman (1990), the portfolio is rapidly becoming the most popular used method of assessing writing; offering excellent criteria for teaching and evaluation. Not all educators and experts agree, however. Hambleton and Murphy (1992) for instance, question the validity and reliability of authentic assessment while stressing that research on new forms of assessment are necessary.

Statement of the Problem

The purpose of this study was to investigate the effects of portfolio assessment on the writing achievement of fourth-grade students. Portfolio assessment was defined as a form of authentic assessment in which the student is required to complete a body of writing over a prolonged period of time.

Review of Related Literature

In recent years the processes of writing instruction and learning to write have drastically changed as researchers and teachers concentrate their attention on the steps used by students instead of on the final written product (Farmer, 1986). Entire school systems have been experimenting with the use of portfolios for writing assessment. The Vermont Portfolio Project (Abruscato, 1993) and the Illinois Writing Program (Chapman, 1990) are two examples of continuing research that support this idea. Both approaches are very similar in structure and assessment criteria, and reports for both efforts indicate promising results in terms of writing performance. These results are supported by other efforts. Marchensi (1992), for instance, found that involvement in a portfolio practicum at the middle school level increased both student participation in writing and attitudes toward the writing process.

Although validity and reliability continue to be a problem, the approach shows promise. Farmer (1986), for example, compared process (portfolio) and traditional approaches to large-scale writing assessment and investigated the magnitude, reliability and validity of scores. Results indicated that the quality of writing was high for both groups but considerably higher for the portfolio group. Interrater reliability was moderate regardless of assessment method but significantly lower for the portfolio group, and concurrent validity was low for both methods but not significantly different between methods.

Statement of the Hypothesis

Although there has been some controversy concerning the use of portfolio assessment as a valid, reliable method for assessing a student's performance in writing, the literature suggests that use of this form of assessment is effective. Therefore, it was hypothesized that fourth-grade students who participate in a portfolio assessment program exhibit better performance in writing than those fourth-grade students who participate in a traditional assessment program.

## Method

Subjects

The sample for this study was selected from the total population of 83 fourth-grade students at an upper-middle-class, private elementary school in Miami, Florida. The population is approximately 65% Hispanic, 30% Caucasian non-Hispanic, and 5% Black American. Using a table of random numbers, 56 students were randomly selected and randomly assigned to 2 groups of 28 each.

Instrument

In this study, the Test of Written Language (TOWL) was used as the measuring instrument. The TOWL was designed for grades 3-12 and is suitable for testing both individuals and groups of students. The main purpose of the TOWL is to fill a void in the assessment of written language and its subskills. It consists of six subtests: 1) vocabulary; 2) thematic maturity; 3) spelling; 4) word usage; 5) style (capitalization & punctuation); and 6) handwriting. Three of the six subtests (handwriting, vocabulary, and thematic maturity) are based on the assessment of a spontaneous writing sample. The three subtests not based on the writing sample (spelling, word usage, and style) consist of the typical multiple choice or right/wrong type of item questions common to other written language achievement tests. The findings of a well conducted assessment effort can be used to: 1) identify students who perform significantly more poorly than their peers in written expression and who as a result need special help; 2) determine a student's particular strengths and weaknesses in various writing abilities; 3) document a student's progress in a special writing program; and 4) conduct research in writing. This instrument was administered in one session lasting 40 minutes.

Although no coefficients are reported for validity, the authors provide an extensive discussion of questions related to the validity of the test. According to

Polloway (1985, p.1602), "content validity is based on the acceptance of the model used for the test and the subsequent selection of items; rationales are provided for both concerns and no significant problems are noted in this area". Criterion validity was determined through correlation with the Myklebust's (1965) Picture Story Language Test (PSLT), the Test of Adolescent Language (TOAL), the Comprehensive Tests of Basic Skills (CTBS), and the teacher ratings of the TOWL's space story. Concurrent validity data with the PSLT is based on the administration of both instruments to a group of elementary students, and although the resulting correlations are generally statistically significant, the author suggests that they must be viewed cautiously since a number of researchers have questioned the PSLT's validity and reliability. Data on predictive validity are not presented.

Reliability data on the TOWL is presented for internal consistency, test-retest reliability, interscorer reliability, and standard error of measurement. Internal consistency reliability of the subtests was determined using the split-half method, corrected with the Spearman-Brown formula. The sample consisted of 432 elementary students at different grade levels, and all coefficients reached or exceeded .80 and were statistically significant. Test-retest reliability data are presented from three studies where students were retested after 2, 3, and 4 weeks respectively; the resulting coefficients ranged from .62 to .90 for the 6 subtests. The coefficients for interscorer reliability were .93 for thematic maturity; .98 for vocabulary; and .76 for handwriting. Standard error of measurement data are reported for age level 12 based on the same data obtained for test-retest reliability.

Direction for the administration and scoring of the TOWL are presented in a clear and concise manner. No significant problems are encountered which might be caused by vague instructions to either examiners or students. And, although all users of this instrument will undoubtedly have suggestions for modifying and improving TOWL, Polloway (1985, p. 1602) states that it "offers the most structurally sound and instructionally relevant instrument currently available in the area of written language."

Experimental Design

The design used in this study was the posttest-only control group design (see figure 1). This design was chosen on the premise that random assignment to group was feasible, and a pretest was not necessary since all students in the study had been previously administered the Test of Written English and scores were available. Choosing this particular design eliminated the majority of threats posed to the internal and external validity of the study. Mortality, a potential threat to internal validity in this design, was not a problem due to the duration of the study (eight weeks) and the consistency of both groups throughout the course of the study.

| Group | Assignment | n | Treatment | Posttest |
|---|---|---|---|---|
| 1 | Random | 28 | Portfolio Assessment Program | TOWL[a] |
| 2 | Random | 28 | Traditional Assessment Program | TOWL |

[a]Test of Written Language

Figure 1. Experimental design.

Procedure

Prior to the beginning of the second marking period for the 1993-1994 school year, 56 of the 83 fourth-grade students were randomly selected and randomly assigned to 2 groups of 28 each. Each group represented a creative writing class which third through sixth graders are requires to take during their second marking period. One of the classes was randomly chosen to participate in the portfolio instruction program. Two of the three creative writing teachers were randomly selected and randomly assigned to one of the classes. Both teachers were female with similar teaching experience, and familiar with authentic assessment approaches.

The study was designed to last eight weeks (one marking period), officially beginning on the first day of the second marking period. The teacher of the control group taught creative writing using the traditional method of instruction. This included lecturing and instruction on the subject matter, and class discussion of students' writing pieces. Her main role was to provide a guide on how to accomplish each of the different writing tasks, such as , how to write a short story, a poem, a letter, and so forth. Each student was graded on the performance of each finished product.

The approach used by the teacher of the experimental group was similar to that of the control group to the extent that she too included lecturing on the subject matter and held class discussions on students' writing pieces. The main difference makes itself evident in the approach or process of how the student accomplished each writing task. For instance, each student kept a portfolio or a history of each writing assignment. This included rough drafts and revisions, with personal feedback from the teacher providing suggestions for improvement before the final work was due. Each student was graded not only on the finished product but on the writing process as well.

Throughout the duration of the study, each class covered the same material, used the same text, and the writing assignments were the same in number and context. Each class met early in the morning for 55 minutes.

In order to compare their writing skills, the TOWL was administered to both classes on the last day of the marking period.

## Results

A $t$ test for independent samples ( $\alpha$ = .05) was used to compare the posttest results of the experimental and control groups. This statistical technique was utilized because it was believed that assumptions required for use of a parametric test were met, e.g., subjects were randomly assigned to groups. It was found that the means of the two groups differed significantly (see Table 1). Therefore, the original hypothesis that "fourth-grade students who participate in a portfolio assessment program exhibit better performance in writing than those fourth-grade students who participate in a traditional assessment program" were supported.

Table 1

Posttest Means, Standard Deviations, and $t$ Tests for the Experimental and Control Groups

| | Group | | |
|---|---|---|---|
| | Portfolio assessment[a] | Traditional assessment[a] | $t$ |
| $M$ | 92.54 | 82.18 | 5.23* |
| $SD$ | 5.68 | 8.80 | |

Note. Maximum score = 110

[a] $n$ = 28
*$p$< .05.

## Discussion

The results of this study support the original hypothesis: Fourth-graders who participated in a portfolio assessment program exhibited better performance in writing achievement than those fourth-graders who participated in a traditional assessment program. The results were not only statistically significant, but also practically significant; portfolio assessment students scored approximately 10 points higher than the traditional assessment students.

The results are consistent with the opinions and findings of Abruscato (1993), Chapman (1990), Farmer (1986), Kennedy (1992), Marchensi (1992), and Winograd & Jones (1992) concerning the positive effects of portfolio assessment on writing achievement. The results, however, cannot be generalized to all classrooms since the study took place in multicultural environment; but the study suggests that portfolio assessment could be equally or more effective in more homogeneous groups as well. Therefore, it is recommended that more studies be effectuated in a variety of settings to determine the true value of portfolio assessment with respect to writing achievement.

## References

Abruscato, J. (1993). Early results and tentative implications from the Vermont portfolio project. Phi Delta Kappan, 74, 474-477.

Chapman, C. (1990). Authentic writing assessment. (Report No. TM-016-137). Washington, DC: American Institutes for Research. (ERIC Document Reproduction Service No. ED 328 606)

Darling-Hammond, L. (1994). Performance-based assessment and educational equity. Harvard Educational Review, 64(1), 5-26.

Farmer, M. (1986). A comparison of process and traditional approaches to large-scale writing assessment: Investigating score magnitude, interrater reliability, and concurrent validity. Dissertation Abstracts International,47, 158A. (University Microfilms No. DA8605264)

Feur, M. J., & Fulton, K. (1993). The many faces of performance assessment. Phi Delta Kappan, 74, 478.

Hambleton, R. K., & Murphy, E. (1992). A psychometric perspective on authentic measurement. Applied Measurement in Education, 5, 1-16.

Kennedy, R. (1992). What is performance assessment? New Directions for Education Reform, 1, 21-27.

Marchensi, R. J. (1992). Using portfolios for more authentic assessment of writing ability. (Report No. CS-213-456). Practicum paper, Nova University. (ERIC Document Reproduction Service No. ED 347 555)

Polloway, E. A. (1985). Review of Test of Written Language. The ninth mental measurements yearbook (pp. 1600-1602). Highland Park, NJ: Gryphon.

Popham, J. W. (1993). Educational testing in America: What's right, what's wrong? A criterion-referenced perspective. Educational Measurement: Issues and Practice, 12, 11-14.

Winograd, P., & Jones, D. L. (1992). The use of portfolios in performance assessment. New Directions for Education Reform, 1,(2), 37-50.

Worthen, B.R. (1993). Critical issues that will determine the future of alternative assessment. Phi Delta Kappan, 74, 444-454.

# PART NINE

## RESEARCH CRITIQUES

**Task 9**

Given a reprint of a research report and an evaluation form, evaluate the components of the report.

Task 9 entails application of a number of questions to the evaluation of an actual research report. In order to give you practice in evaluating a research study, one of the reports presented in Part One, Reading Time in School: Effect on Fourth Graders' Performance on a Criterion-Referenced Comprehension Test, has been evaluated for you. Following this discussion, questions are listed for you to answer with respect to that article. In answering the questions, use the following codes:

Y = Yes
N = No
NA = Not applicable
?/X = Can't tell/Don't know

When appropriate, as you answer the questions, underline components which correspond to questions to which you have responded "Y". For example, if you decide that there is a statement of the problem, underline it in the article. Since the study which you are going to evaluate is experimental, you are also asked to identify and diagram the experimental design used. If your responses match reasonably well with those given in the Suggested Responses, you are probably ready for Task 9. Make sure that you understand the reason for any discrepancies, especially on questions for which responses are less judgmental and more objective; adequacy of the literature review is more judgmental whereas the presence or absence of a hypothesis can be objectively determined.

# Self-Test For Task 9

### Reading time in School: Effect on Fourth Graders' Performance on a Criterion-Referenced Comprehension Test

GENERAL EVALUATION CRITERIA

Introduction

| <u>Problem</u> | CODE |
|---|---|
| Is there a statement of the problem? | ____ |
| Is the problem "researchable"? | ____ |
| Is background information on the problem presented? | ____ |
| Is the educational significance of the problem discussed? | ____ |
| Does the problem statement indicate the variables of interest and the specific relationship between those variables which was investigated? | ____ |
| When necessary, are variables directly or operationally defined? | ____ |
| <u>Review of Related Literature</u> | |
| Is the review comprehensive? | ____ |
| Are all references cited relevant to the problem under investigation? | ____ |
| Are most of the sources primary, i.e., are there only a few or no secondary sources? | ____ |
| Have the references been critically analyzed and the results of various studies compared and contrasted, i.e., is the review more than a series of abstracts or annotations? | ____ |
| Is the review well-organized? Does it logically flow in such a way that the references least related to the problem are discussed first and the most related references are discussed last? | ____ |
| Does the review conclude with a brief summary of the literature and its implications for the problem investigated? | ____ |
| Do the implications discussed form an empirical or theoretical rationale for the hypotheses which follow? | ____ |
| <u>Hypotheses</u> | |
| Are specific questions to be answered listed or specific hypotheses to be tested stated? | ____ |
| Does each hypothesis state an expected relationship or difference? | ____ |
| If necessary, are variables directly or operationally defined? | ____ |
| Is each hypothesis testable? | |

## Method

### Subjects

CODE

Are the size and major characteristics of the population studied described? ____

If a sample was selected, is the method of selecting the sample clearly described? ____

Is the method of sample selection described one that is likely to result in a representative, unbiased sample? ____

Did the researcher avoid the use of volunteers? ____

Are the size and major characteristics of the sample described? ____

Does the sample size meet the suggested guidelines for minimum sample size appropriate for the method of research represented? ____

### Instruments

Is a rationale given for the selection of the instruments (or measurements) used? ____

Is each instrument described in terms of purpose and content? ____

Are the instruments appropriate for measuring the intended variables? ____

Is evidence presented that indicates that each instrument is appropriate for the sample under study? ____

Is instrument validity discussed and coefficients given if appropriate? ____

Is reliability discussed in terms of type and size of reliability coefficients? ____

If appropriate, are subtest reliabilities given? ____

If an instrument was developed specifically for the study, are the procedures involved in its development and validation described? ____

If an instrument was developed specifically for the study, are administration, scoring or tabulating, and interpretation procedures fully described? ____

### Design and Procedure

Is the design appropriate for testing the hypotheses of the study? ____

Are procedures described in sufficient detail to permit replication by another researcher? ____

If a pilot study was conducted, are its execution and results described as well as its impact on the subsequent study? ____

Are control procedures described? ____

Did the researcher discuss or account for any potentially confounding variables that he or she was unable to control for? ____

| Results | CODE |
|---|---|
| Are appropriate descriptive statistics presented? | ___ |
| Was the probability level, __, at which the results of the tests of significance were evaluated, specified in advance of data analysis? | ___ |
| If parametric tests were used, is there evidence that the researcher avoided violating the required assumptions for parametric tests? | ___ |
| Are the tests of significance described appropriate, given the hypotheses and design of the study? | ___ |
| Was every hypothesis tested? | ___ |
| Are the tests of significance interpreted using the appropriate degrees of freedom? | ___ |
| Are the results clearly presented? | ___ |
| Are the tables and figures (if any) well organized and easy to understand? | ___ |
| Are the data in each table and figure described in the text? | ___ |

## Discussion (Conclusions and Recommendations)

| | |
|---|---|
| Is each result discussed in terms of the original hypothesis to which it relates? | ___ |
| Is each result discussed in terms of its agreement or disagreement with previous results obtained by other researchers in other studies? | ___ |
| Are generalizations consistent with the results? | ___ |
| Are the possible effects of uncontrolled variables on the results discussed? | ___ |
| Are the theoretical and practical implications of the findings discussed? | ___ |
| Are recommendations for future action made? | ___ |
| Are the suggestions for future action based on practical significance or on statistical significance only, i.e., has the author avoided confusing practical and statistical significance? | ___ |
| Are recommendations for future research made? | ___ |

## Abstract (or Summary)

| | |
|---|---|
| Is the problem restated? | ___ |
| Are the number and type of subjects and instruments described? | ___ |
| Is the design used identified? | ___ |
| Are procedures described? | ___ |
| Are the major results and conclusions restated? | ___ |

## METHOD-SPECIFIC EVALUATION CRITERIA

Identify and diagram the experimental design used in this study:

| | CODE |
|---|---|
| Was an appropriate experimental design selected? | ____ |
| Is a rationale for design selection given? | ____ |
| Are sources of invalidity associated with the design identified and discussed? | ____ |
| Is the method of group formation described? | ____ |
| Was the experimental group formed in the same way as the control group? | ____ |
| Were groups randomly formed and the use of existing groups avoided? | ____ |
| Were treatments randomly assigned to groups? | ____ |
| Were critical extraneous variables identified? | ____ |
| Were any control procedures applied to equate groups on extraneous variables? | ____ |
| Were possible reactive arrangements (e.g., the Hawthorne effect) controlled for? | ____ |

# SUGGESTED RESPONSES

## PART ONE

### SELF-TEST FOR TASK 1-A

#### Reading Time in School: Effect on Fourth Graders' Performance on a Criterion-Referenced Comprehension Test

**The Problem.** The study was designed to explore the impact that a regular and sustained self-selected reading program may have on a selected set of reading skills measured by a criterion-referenced reading skills test.

**The Procedures.** The sample contained 61 fourth-grade students attending a middle to lower class suburban elementary school located in the Rocky Mountain region. A pretest-posttest comparison group design was used. Students were randomly assigned to three comparison groups (reading only, skills only, reading/skills comparison group). The two instruments for the study consisted of the comprehension subtest of a standardized achievement test, the CTBS, and a researcher-designed Specific Comprehension Skills Test (SCST). For 30 days, students participated in their respective treatments for 30 min. per day, and then returned to their intact classrooms for an additional 30 min. of reading and skill lessons.

**The Method of Analysis.** The mean posttest scores for each of the three treatment groups on each of the four comprehensive skill measures were compared using <u>analysis of covariance</u>, with each pretest score serving as the covariate in each of the four separate ANCOVA analyses.

**The Major Conclusion.** The results showed no significant differences among the three treatment groups at the conclusion of the experiment on the posttest form of the Specific Comprehension Skills Test; students made significant and essentially equivalent gains from the pretest to the posttest on four selected reading comprehension skills.

#### Teachers' Use of Homework in High Schools

**The Problem.** The authors attempted to fill in some of the gaps about how homework is used by high school teachers by presenting teacher replies to 14 general questions.

**The Procedures.** At the approximately 700 public high schools in Illinois, 100 were randomly selected and invited to participate; teachers and principles in 92 schools agreed to contribute. Of the 5,092 teachers in these schools, 2,986 teachers returned useable questionnaires, a 59% return rate (which varied from 70% to 52%, depending on school type). A 37-item survey was developed for the study, and the questions were designed to assess activity across five components of homework. Based on pilot studies, the questionnaire was revised several times.

**The Method of Analysis.** All questions were analyzed descriptively and results were presented in terms of frequency of occurrence and percentages (%).

**The Major Conclusion.** Students are completing considerably more homework than they did 10 years ago. The author noted that the path for future studies in the area of homework is becoming more clearly delineated.

## The Accuracy of Principals' Judgments of Teacher Performance

**The Problem.** The study addresses three specific questions:

1. How accurate, on the average, are principals' judgments of the performance of the teachers they supervise?
2. Does the accuracy of principals' judgments of the performance of the teachers they supervise depend on which principal makes the judgments?
3. Is there any relationship between the accuracy of a principal's judgment of the performance of a teacher and a) the grade level the teacher teaches, b) the ability of the student whose achievement gain is measured, or c) the achievement gains as measured in reading or mathematics?

**The Procedures.** Principals' judgments were recorded on a form originally developed and used in an earlier study. Teacher effectiveness in teaching reading and arithmetic was estimated from students' pretest scores and posttest scores on two standardized achievement tests. The sample of teachers used in the study was obtained by first drawing a sample of principals and then using only those teachers whose performance they were willing to rate; 46 principals agreed to participate. The final sample of teachers consisted of 87 groups of elementary-school teachers ($\underline{n}$ = 322).

**The Method of Analysis.** Coefficients of correlation were calculated separately in each of the 87 groups between the 4 ESG's (estimated gain scores) of each teacher and the principal's judgment of the teacher's performance of each of the three roles.

**The Major Conclusions.** The most important finding of this study is the low accuracy of the average principal's judgments of the performance of the teachers he or she supervises. The second major outcome of this study was the failure to find evidence that principals vary in their ability to judge teacher performance. The third finding is that the accuracy of judgments of teacher performance is related to the grade level taught by the teacher whose performance is being judged.

## Reflective Thinking and Growth in Novices' Teaching Abilities

**The Problem.** Since there is no reported research that specifically examines prospective teachers' reflective thoughts in relation to improved teaching abilities over the course of a semester, the study was conducted to formally explore that assumptive theme.

**The Procedures.** The participants were 23 female elementary education majors enrolled in two reading/language arts methods courses designated as an early field experience. Seminar discussions focused upon novices' teaching concerns; however, existing school policies and practices also were considered in relation to socio/political realities. Each week, for 15 weeks, the prospective teachers wrote their thoughts and feelings about teaching in their journals. Each week the program supervisor read the journals and then wrote feedback comments designed to encourage the novices to reflect in their journals. Each novice teacher prepared and taught four lessons weekly; the lessons were informally but attentively observed over the semester by the participating classroom teachers (N=16) and were formally observed by the program supervisor.

**The Method of Analysis.** Initial ratings of novices' teaching abilities, independently made by the classroom teachers and program supervisor, were averaged and compared with their final averages. Additionally, two university supervisors who use dialogue journals on a regular basis with their own students, scored the novices' reflective journal statements.

**The Major Conclusion.** Although it is premature to conclude that the more prospective teachers reflect about their work, the more their teaching abilities will improve, the results of the study suggest that the assumptive theme that links prospective teachers' reflective thinking to their teaching is an appropriate assumption.

## Classroom Behavior of Good and Poor Readers

**The Problem.** The purpose of the study was to provide consistency by investigating a single set of objectively observable behavior of both good and poor readers in classroom settings from Grades 1 through 11.

**The Procedures.** Subjects were 108 public school students enrolled in regular classes from grades 1, 3, 5, 7, 9, and 11. The 3 best and 3 worst readers in each of three classrooms at each of 6 grade levels were chosen as subjects. Based on a review of literature, discussion with classroom teachers, and review of methods for objectively observing students behavior in classroom settings, specific behaviors likely to differentiate good from poor readers were chosen. From the original set of specific behaviors, seven were chosen that could be consistently identified and precisely defined: seconds to start, materials missing, noise, out of place, physical contact or destruction, off task, and volunteering. Pilot sessions continued until a reliability of 90% was attained by independent observers recording the behavior of the same students at the same time. Each classroom was observed for 30 min. a day for 10 days.

**The Method of Analysis.** The data were analyzed using a two-way analysis of variance (ANOVA) procedure.

**The Major Conclusions.** No significant differences were found between good and poor readers in starting to work on assignments, having necessary materials available, making unacceptable noise, being out of place, or making unacceptable contact with other persons or their property. Significant differences were found in attending to instructional tasks and volunteering to participate; poor readers attended less and volunteered less.

## SELF-TEST FOR TASK 1-B

### Reading Time in School: Effect on Fourth Graders' Performance on a Criterion-Referenced Comprehension Test

**Type:** Experimental

**Reasons:** A cause-effect relationship was investigated. The independent variable (cause), reading time (reading only versus skills only versus a reading/skills combination), was manipulated. Subjects were randomly assigned to one of the three groups. The subjects' performance on the dependent variable (a criterion-referenced comprehension skills test) was compared.

### Teachers' Use of Homework in High Schools

**Type:** Descriptive

**Reasons:** The authors provided information about how homework is used by high school teachers by presenting teacher replies to 14 general questions. The study did not investigate a cause-effect relationship or a correlational relationship, nor did it investigate past events.

### The Accuracy of Principals' Judgments of Teacher Performance

**Type:** Correlational

**Reasons:** A cause-effect relationship was not investigated. A relationship was investigated - the relationship between teachers' estimated gain scores and principals' judgment of their performance. Correlation coefficients were computed.

### Reflective Thinking and Growth in Novices' Teaching Abilities

**Method:** Qualitative

**Reasons:** Field research methodology was used, specifically analysis of reflective journals and multiple observations coupled with some descriptive statistics.

### Classroom Behavior of Good and Poor Readers

**Type:** Causal-Comparative

**Reasons:** A cause-effect relationship was investigated. The independent variable (cause), reading ability (good versus poor), was not manipulated. The best and worst readers were identified by examining the latest standardized reading achievement test scores or kindergarten teachers' ratings. Specific behaviors (the dependent variable) of the good and poor readers were compared.

## PART TWO

### Exercise II-1

1. At-risk eighth graders who participate in a self-esteem course earn higher grade point averages than at-risk eighth graders who do not participate in a self-esteem course.

2. College-level introductory psychology students who take short-answer tests have greater retention of psychological concepts and principles than college-level introductory psychology students who take multiple-choice tests.

3. Public school students who graduate have higher incomes at age 25 than public school students who drop out of school prior to graduation.

4. Third-grade students who use manipulative materials during mathematics instruction exhibit greater achievement in math than third-grade students who do not use manipulatives.

5. Tenth-grade biology students who perform dissection in their lab have less positive attitudes toward biology than 10th-grade biology students who manipulate models.

### Exercise II-2

1. There is no difference in the grade point averages of at-risk eighth graders who participate in a self-esteem course and those who do not participate in a self-esteem course.

2. There is no difference in the retention of psychological concepts and principles of college-level introductory psychology students who take short-answer tests and those who take multiple-choice tests.

3. There is no difference in the income at age 25 of public school students who graduate and those who drop out prior to graduation.

4. There is no difference in math achievement between third-grade students who use manipulative materials during mathematics instruction and third-grade students who do not use manipulatives.

5. There is no difference in the attitudes toward biology of 10th-grade biology students who perform dissection in their lab and 10th-grade biology students who manipulate models.

---

## PART FOUR

### Exercise IV-1

1. There are 150 first graders in the population and you want a random sample of 60 students.

    1) Compile or obtain a list of the 150 first graders.
    2) Assign each subject a number from 000-149.
    3) Go to a table of random numbers and arbitrarily select a number.
    4) Look at the last 3 digits of the numbers.
    5) If that number is also assigned to a subject, that subject is in the sample; if not, go to the next number.
    6) Continue down the table until 60 students are selected.

2. There are 220 principals in the school system and you want a random sample of 40 principals.

   1) Compile or obtain a list of the 220 principals.
   2) Assign each principal a number from 000-219.
   3) Go to a table of random number and arbitrarily select a number.
   4) Look at the last 3 digits of the number.
   5) If that number is also assigned to a subject, that subject is in the sample; if not go to the next number.
   6) Continue down the table until 40 principals are selected.

3. There are 320 students defined as gifted in the school system and you want a random sample of 50 gifted students.

   1) Compile or obtain a list of the 320 gifted students.
   2) Assign each gifted student a number from 000-319.
   3) Go to a table of random numbers and arbitrarily select a number.
   4) Look at the last 3 digits of the number.
   5) If that number is also assigned to a subject, that subject is in the sample; if not go to the next number.
   6) Continue down the table until 50 gifted students are selected.

**Exercise IV-2**

1. There are 500 12th-grade students in the population, you want a sample of 60 students, and you want to stratify on 3 levels of IQ in order to insure equal representation.

   1) Administer an IQ test (or otherwise obtain IQ scores) and classify all students into one of 3 IQ groups (e.g., those with an IQ below 84, those with IQ between 84 and 116, and those with an IQ above 116).
   2) Randomly select 20 students from each IQ group.

2. There are 95 algebra I students in the population, you want a sample of 30 students, and you want to stratify on sex in order to insure equal representation of males and females.

   1) Classify all the algebra I students as male or female.
   2) Randomly select 15 males and 15 females.

3. There are 240 principals in the school system, you want a sample of 45 principals, and you want to stratify by level, i.e., elementary versus secondary, in order to insure proportional representation. You know that there are approximately twice as many secondary principals as elementary principals.

   1) Identify all the elementary principals and all the secondary principals.
   2) Randomly select 15 elementary principals and 30 secondary principals; this will give you a sample of 45 which contains twice as many secondary principals as elementary principals.

**Exercise IV-3**

1. There are 80 6th-grade classrooms in the population, each classroom has an average of 30 students, and you want a sample of 180 students.

   1) The number of classrooms needed $= \frac{180}{30} = 6.$
   2) Randomly select 6 classrooms from the population of 80 classrooms.
   3) All the 6th graders in the 6 classrooms selected are in the sample.

2. There are 75 schools in the school system, each school has an average of 50 teachers, and you want a sample of 350 teachers.

   1) The number of schools needed $= \frac{350}{50} = 7.$
   2) Randomly select 7 schools from the population of 75 schools.
   3) All the teachers in the 7 schools selected are in the sample.

3. There are 100 kindergarten classes in the school system, each class has an average of 20 children, and you want a sample of 200 children.

   1) The number of kindergarten classes needed $= \frac{200}{20} = 10.$
   2) Randomly select 10 kindergartens from the population of 100 kindergarten classes.
   3) All the children in the 10 classes selected are in the sample.

**Exercise IV-4**

1. You have a list of 2,000 high school students and you want a sample of 200 students.

   1) $K = \frac{2{,}000}{20} = 10.$
   2) Arbitrarily select a name at the top of the list.
   3) Select every 10th name on the list until you have selected 200 students.

2. You have a directory which lists the names and addresses of 12,000 teachers and you want a sample of 2,500 teachers.

   1) $K = \frac{12{,}000}{2{,}500} = 4.8$ or 5.
   2) Arbitrarily select a name at the beginning of the directory.
   3) Select every 5th name in the directory until you have selected 2,500 teachers.

3. You have a list of 1,500 junior high school students and you want a sample of 100 students.

1) $K = \frac{1,500}{100} = 15.$

2) Arbitrarily select a name at the top of the list.

3) Select every 15th name until you have selected 100 students.

---

## PART FIVE

**Exercise V-1**

1.A 2.D 3.C 4.A 5.B

**Exercise V-2**

1.C 2.A 3.B 4.D 5.C

**Exercise V-3**

1. You want to determine the concurrent validity of a new IQ test for young children.

   1) Obtain scores on an already established, valid IQ test for a large group of young children (or administer such a test if scores are not already available).
   2) Administer the new IQ test to the same group.
   3) Correlate the two sets of scores.
   4) If the correlation is high, the new test has high concurrent validity with the already established test.

2. You want to determine the concurrent validity of a new self-concept scale for junior high school students.

   1) Obtain scores on an already established, valid self-concept scale for a large group of junior high school students (or administer such a test if scores are not already available).
   2) Administer the new self-concept scale to the same group.
   3) Correlate the two sets of scores.
   4) If the correlation is high, the new scale has high concurrent validity with the already established scale.

5. You want to determine the concurrent validity of a new reading comprehension test for high school students.

   1) Obtain scores on an already established, valid test of reading comprehension for a large group of high school students (or administer such a test if scores are not already available).
   2) Administer the new reading comprehension test to the same group.
   3) Correlate the two sets of scores.
   4) If the correlation is high, the new scale has high concurrent validity with the already established test.

**Exercise V-4**

1. You want to predict success in graduate school and you want to determine the predictive validity of the GRE.

    1) Administer the GRE to a large group of students entering graduate school.
    2) Collect data on the criterion measure, a valid index of success in graduate school such as GPA at the time of graduation.
    3) Correlate the two sets of data.
    4) If the correlation is high, the GRE has high predictive validity with respect to success in graduate school.

2. You want to predict level of achievement in algebra I and you want to determine the predictive validity of an algebra I aptitude test.

    1) Administer the algebra aptitude test to a large group of students who are going to take algebra I.
    2) Collect data on the criterion measure, a valid index of level of achievement in algebra I such as final exam scores or final average.
    3) Correlate the two sets of data.
    4) If the correlation is high, the algebra I aptitude test has high predictive validity with respect to level of achievement in algebra I.

3. You want to predict success in nursing school and you want to determine the predictive validity of a nursing aptitude test.

    1) Administer the nursing aptitude test to a large group of students who are entering nursing school.
    2) Collect data on the criterion measure, a valid index of success in nursing school such as scores on a final performance test.
    3) Correlate the two sets of scores.
    4) If the correlation is high, the nursing aptitude test has high predictive validity with respect to success in nursing school.

---

## PART SIX

**Exercise VI-1**

1.G 2.J 3.A 4.E 5.C

**Exercise VI-2**

1.H 2.H 3.C 4.E 5.D

---

## PART SEVEN

**Exercise VII-1**

1.D 2.B 3.F 4.G 5.A

EXERCISE VII - 2

| $X$ | $X^2$ |
|---|---|
| 2 | 4 |
| 4 | 16 |
| 4 | 16 |
| 5 | 25 |
| 6 | 36 |
| 6 | 36 |
| 6 | 36 |
| 7 | 49 |
| 8 | 64 |
| 9 | 81 |
| $\sum X = 57$ | $\sum X^2 = 363$ |

---

$$\bar{X} = \frac{\sum X}{N} = \frac{57}{10} = \underline{\underline{5.7}}$$

$$SD = \sqrt{\frac{\sum X^2 - \frac{(\sum X)^2}{N}}{N - 1}} = \sqrt{\frac{363 - \frac{(57)^2}{10}}{9}} = \sqrt{\frac{363 - \frac{3249}{10}}{9}}$$

$$= \sqrt{\frac{363 - 324.9}{9}} = \sqrt{\frac{38.1}{9}} = \sqrt{4.23} = \underline{\underline{2.06}}$$

| $X$ | $Y$ | $X^2$ | $Y^2$ | $XY$ |
|---|---|---|---|---|
| 2 | 6 | 4 | 36 | 12 |
| 4 | 6 | 16 | 36 | 24 |
| 4 | 7 | 16 | 49 | 28 |
| 5 | 8 | 25 | 64 | 40 |
| 6 | 9 | 36 | 81 | 54 |
| 21 | 36 | 97 | 266 | 158 |
| $\sum X$ | $\sum Y$ | $\sum X^2$ | $\sum Y^2$ | $\sum XY$ |

$$r = \frac{\sum XY - \frac{(\sum X)(\sum Y)}{N}}{\sqrt{\left[\sum X^2 - \frac{(\sum X)^2}{N}\right]\left[\sum Y^2 - \frac{(\sum Y)^2}{N}\right]}} = \frac{158 - \frac{(21)(36)}{5}}{\sqrt{\left[97 - \frac{(21)^2}{5}\right]\left[266 - \frac{(36)^2}{5}\right]}}$$

$$= \frac{158 - \frac{756}{5}}{\sqrt{\left[97 - \frac{441}{5}\right]\left[266 - \frac{(1296)}{5}\right]}} = \frac{158 - 151.2}{\sqrt{\left[97 - 88.2\right]\left[266 - 259.2\right]}}$$

$$= \frac{6.8}{\sqrt{[8.8]\,[6.8]}} = \frac{6.8}{\sqrt{59.84}} = \frac{6.8}{7.74} = .8786$$

$$r = \underline{\underline{.88}}$$

$$z_1 = \frac{X - \bar{X}}{SD} = \frac{2 - 5.7}{2.06}$$

$$= \frac{-3.7}{2.06} = \underline{\underline{-1.80}}$$

$$z_2 = \frac{X - \bar{X}}{SD} = \frac{4 - 5.7}{2.06}$$

$$= \frac{-1.7}{2.06} = \underline{\underline{-.83}}$$

$$z_3 = \frac{X - \bar{X}}{SD} = \frac{4 - 5.7}{2.06}$$

$$= \frac{-1.7}{2.06} = \underline{\underline{-.83}}$$

$$z_4 = \frac{X - \bar{X}}{SD} = \frac{5 - 5.7}{2.06}$$

$$= \frac{-.7}{2.06} = \underline{\underline{-.34}}$$

$$z_5 = \frac{X - \bar{X}}{SD} = \frac{6 - 5.7}{2.06}$$

$$\frac{.3}{2.06} = \underline{\underline{+.15}}$$

$$z_6 = \frac{X - \bar{X}}{SD} = \frac{6 - 5.7}{2.06}$$

$$= \frac{.3}{2.06} = \underline{\underline{+.15}}$$

$$z_7 = \frac{X - \bar{X}}{SD} = \frac{6 - 5.7}{2.06}$$

$$= \frac{.3}{2.06} = \underline{\underline{+.15}}$$

$$z_8 = \frac{X - \bar{X}}{SD} = \frac{7 - 5.7}{2.06}$$

$$= \frac{1.3}{2.06} = \underline{\underline{+.63}}$$

$$z_9 = \frac{X - \bar{X}}{SD} = \frac{8 - 5.7}{2.06}$$

$$= \frac{2.3}{2.06} = \underline{\underline{+1.12}}$$

$$z_{10} = \frac{X - \bar{X}}{SD} = \frac{9 - 5.7}{2.06}$$

$$= \frac{3.3}{2.06} = \underline{\underline{+1.60}}$$

| $X_1$ | $X_2$ | $X_3$ |
|---|---|---|
| 2 | 3 | 7 |
| 3 | 3 | 8 |
| 4 | 4 | 8 |
| 5 | 5 | 8 |
| 7 | 6 | 9 |

---

$\underline{t}$ test for independent samples

| $x_1$ | $x_1^2$ | $x_2$ | $x_2^2$ |
|---|---|---|---|
| 2 | 4 | 3 | 9 |
| 3 | 9 | 3 | 9 |
| 4 | 16 | 4 | 16 |
| 5 | 25 | 5 | 25 |
| 7 | 49 | 6 | 36 |
| 21 | 103 | 21 | 95 |
| $\Sigma x_1$ | $\Sigma x_1^2$ | $\Sigma x_2$ | $\Sigma x_2^2$ |

$$\overline{X}_1 = \frac{\Sigma X_1}{n_1} = \frac{21}{5} = 4.2 \qquad \overline{X}_2 = \frac{\Sigma X_2}{n_2} = \frac{21}{5} = 4.2$$

$SS_1 = \Sigma X_1^2 - \frac{(\Sigma X_1)^2}{n_1}$

$= 103 - \frac{(21)^2}{5}$

$= 103 - \frac{441}{5}$

$= 103 - 88.2$

$= 14.8$

$SS_2 = \Sigma X_2^2 - \frac{(\Sigma X_2)^2}{n_2}$

$= 95 - \frac{(21)^2}{5}$

$= 95 - \frac{441}{5}$

$= 95 - 88.2$

$= 6.8$

$$\underline{t} = \frac{\overline{X}_1 - \overline{X}_2}{\sqrt{\left(\frac{SS_1 + SS_2}{n_1 + n_2 - 2}\right)\left(\frac{1}{n_1} + \frac{1}{n_2}\right)}} = \frac{4.2 - 4.2}{\sqrt{\left(\frac{14.8 + 6.8}{5 + 5 - 2}\right)\left(\frac{1}{5} + \frac{1}{5}\right)}}$$

$$= \frac{0}{\sqrt{\left(\frac{21.6}{8}\right)\left(\frac{2}{5}\right)}} = \frac{0}{\sqrt{(2.7)(.4)}} = \frac{0}{\sqrt{1.08}} = \frac{0}{1.04} = 0$$

$\underline{t} = 0$

$\underline{df} = n_1 + n_2 - 2 = 5 + 5 - 2 = 8$

$\alpha = .05$

$\underline{t} = 0$ is less than 2.306 (See Table A.4)

Therefore, there is no significant difference between the two groups.

$\underline{t}$ test for nonindependent samples

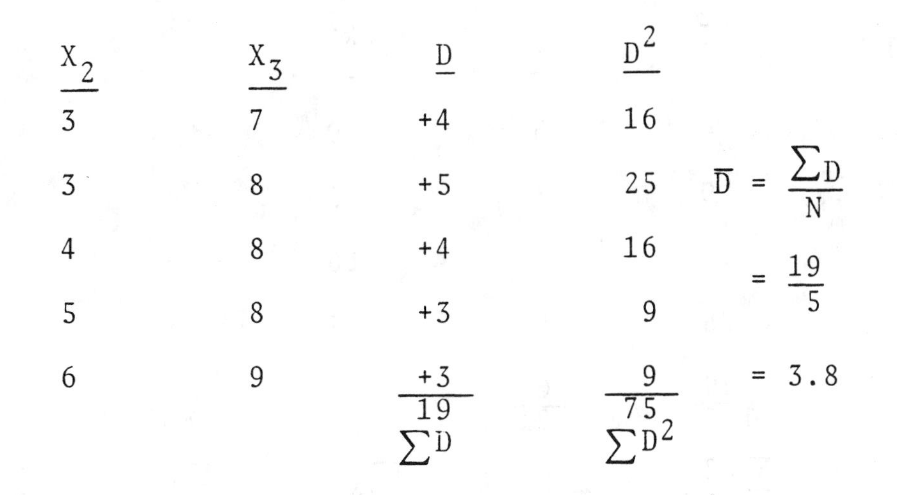

| $X_2$ | $X_3$ | D | $D^2$ |
|---|---|---|---|
| 3 | 7 | +4 | 16 |
| 3 | 8 | +5 | 25 |
| 4 | 8 | +4 | 16 |
| 5 | 8 | +3 | 9 |
| 6 | 9 | +3 | 9 |
| | | 19 | 75 |
| | | $\sum D$ | $\sum D^2$ |

$$\bar{D} = \frac{\sum D}{N} = \frac{19}{5} = 3.8$$

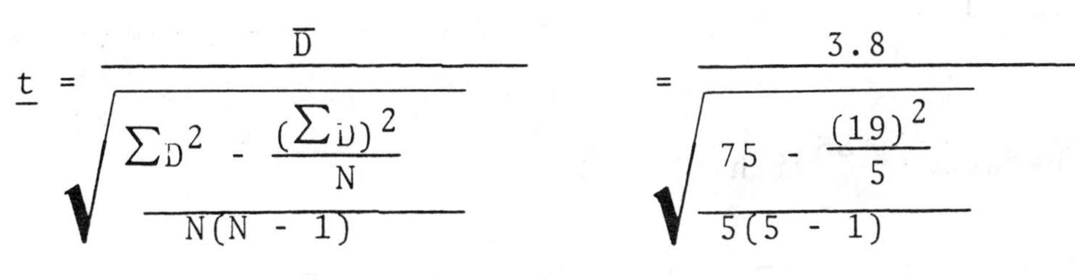

$$\underline{t} = \frac{\bar{D}}{\sqrt{\dfrac{\sum D^2 - \dfrac{(\sum D)^2}{N}}{N(N-1)}}} = \frac{3.8}{\sqrt{\dfrac{75 - \dfrac{(19)^2}{5}}{5(5-1)}}}$$

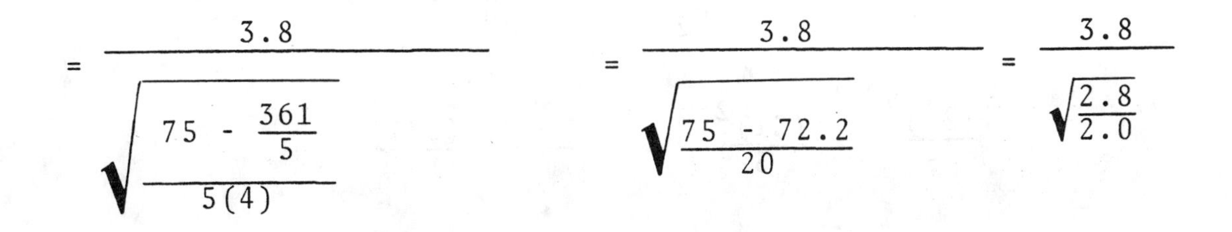

$$= \frac{3.8}{\sqrt{\dfrac{75 - \dfrac{361}{5}}{5(4)}}} = \frac{3.8}{\sqrt{\dfrac{75 - 72.2}{20}}} = \frac{3.8}{\sqrt{\dfrac{2.8}{2.0}}}$$

$$= \frac{3.8}{\sqrt{.14}} = \frac{3.8}{.37} = 10.27$$

$\underline{t} = 10.27$; $\underline{df} = n - 1 = 5 - 1 = 4$; $\alpha = .05$

$\underline{t} = 10.27$ is greater than 2.776 (See Table A.4)

Therefore, there is a significant difference between the two groups.

Simple analysis of variance for 3 groups

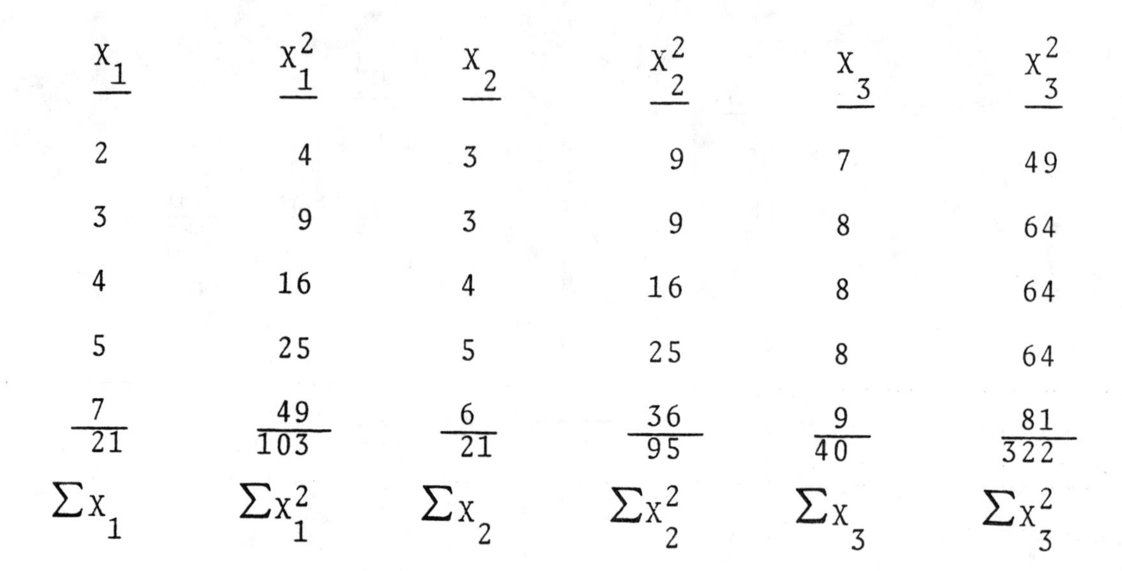

| $X_1$ | $X_1^2$ | $X_2$ | $X_2^2$ | $X_3$ | $X_3^2$ |
|---|---|---|---|---|---|
| 2 | 4 | 3 | 9 | 7 | 49 |
| 3 | 9 | 3 | 9 | 8 | 64 |
| 4 | 16 | 4 | 16 | 8 | 64 |
| 5 | 25 | 5 | 25 | 8 | 64 |
| 7 | 49 | 6 | 36 | 9 | 81 |
| 21 | 103 | 21 | 95 | 40 | 322 |
| $\Sigma X_1$ | $\Sigma X_1^2$ | $\Sigma X_2$ | $\Sigma X_2^2$ | $\Sigma X_3$ | $\Sigma X_3^2$ |

$$SS_{total} = SS_{between} + SS_{within}$$

$$SS_{between} = \frac{(\Sigma X_1)^2}{n_1} + \frac{(\Sigma X_2)^2}{n_2} + \frac{(\Sigma X_3)^2}{n_3} - \frac{(\Sigma X)^2}{N}$$

$$= \frac{(21)^2}{5} + \frac{(21)^2}{5} + \frac{(40)^2}{5} - \frac{(82)^2}{15}$$

$$= \frac{441}{5} + \frac{441}{5} + \frac{1,600}{5} - \frac{6,724}{15}$$

$$= 88.2 + 88.2 + 320 - 448.27$$

$$= 496.4 - 448.27 = \underline{\underline{48.13}}$$

$$SS_{total} = \Sigma X^2 - \frac{(\Sigma X)^2}{N} = 520 - 448.27 = \underline{\underline{71.73}}$$

$$SS_{within} = SS_{total} - SS_{between}$$

$$= 71.73 - 48.13 = \underline{\underline{23.60}}$$

| SOURCE OF VARIATION | SUM OF SQUARES | df | | MEAN SQUARES | F |
|---|---|---|---|---|---|
| Between | 48.13 | (K-1) | 2 | 24.06 | 12.21 |
| Within | 23.60 | (N-K) | 12 | 1.97 | |
| Total | 71.73 | (N-1) | 14 | | |

*F* = 12.21; *df* = 2, 12; $\alpha$ = .05

*F* = 12.21 is greater than 3.88 (See Table A.5)

Therefore, there is a significant difference among the groups.

The Scheffé Test

$$\bar{X}_1 = \frac{\Sigma X_1}{n} = \frac{21}{5} = 4.2$$

$$\bar{X}_2 = \frac{\Sigma X_2}{n_2} = \frac{21}{5} = 4.2$$

$$\bar{X}_3 = \frac{\Sigma X_3}{n_3} = \frac{40}{5} = 8.0$$

$$MS_w = 1.97$$

$(K-1) = 3-1 = 2$ $\qquad$ $(N-K) = 15-3 = 12$

$$\underline{F} = \frac{(\bar{X}_1 - \bar{X}_2)^2}{MS_w\left(\frac{1}{n_1} + \frac{1}{n_2}\right)\left(K - 1\right)} = \frac{0^2}{1.97\ (.4)2} = \frac{0}{1.58} = 0$$

$\underline{F} = 0$, $\underline{df} = 2, 12$, $\underline{p} = .05$, table value $= 3.88$

$0 < 3.88$, therefore there is no significant difference between $\bar{X}_1$ and $\bar{X}_2$

$$\underline{F} = \frac{(\bar{X}_2 - \bar{X}_3)^2}{MS_w\left(\frac{1}{n_1} + \frac{1}{n_2}\right)\left(K - 1\right)} = \frac{(4.2 - 8.0)^2}{1.97\left(\frac{1}{5} + \frac{1}{5}\right)2}$$

$$= \frac{(-3.8)^2}{1.97\ (.4)2}$$

$$= \frac{14.44}{1.58}$$

$$= 9.14$$

$\underline{F} = 9.14$, $\underline{df} = 2.12$, $\alpha = .05$, table value $= 3.88$

9.14 3.88, therefore there <u>is</u> a significant difference between $\bar{X}_2$ and $\bar{X}_3$

Since $\bar{X}_1 = \bar{X}_2$, the calculations for $\bar{X}_1 - \bar{X}_3$ are the same as for $\bar{X}_2 - \bar{X}_3$

Chi square $\chi^2$

Responses

| | Yes | No | Undecided | |
|---|---|---|---|---|
| observed | 21 | 21 | 40 | total: 82 |
| expected | 27.3 | 27.3 | 27.3 | |

(Note: expected $= \frac{82}{3} = 27.3$)

$$\chi^2 = \sum \left[ \frac{(fo - fe)^2}{fe} \right]$$

$$\chi^2 = \frac{(21 - 27.3)^2}{27.3} + \frac{(21 - 27.3)^2}{27.3} + \frac{(40 - 27.3)^2}{27.3}$$

$$= \frac{(-6.3)^2}{27.3} + \frac{(-6.3)^2}{27.3} + \frac{(12.7)^2}{27.3}$$

$$= \frac{39.69}{27.3} + \frac{39.69}{27.3} + \frac{161.29}{27.3}$$

$$= 1.45 + 1.45 + 5.91 = \underline{\underline{8.81}}$$

$\chi^2 = 8.81$; $\underline{df} = K - 1 = 3 - 1 = 2$; $\alpha = .05$

$\chi^2 = 8.81 > 5.991$ (See Table A.6)

Therefore, there is a significant difference between observed and expected frequencies.

THE NUMBER OF SCORES (N) IS 10

THE SUM OF THE SCORES (EX) IS 57

THE MEAN OF THE SCORES ($\bar{X}$) IS 5.7

THE SUM OF THE SQUARED SCORES ($EX^2$) IS 363

THE SUM OF SQUARES (SS) IS 38.1

THE STANDARD DEVIATION FOR A SAMPLE IS 2.06

THE STANDARD DEVIATION FOR A POPULATION IS 1.95

---

THERE WERE 5 PAIRS OF SCORES.

THE PEARSON'S 'r' IS .88

THERE WERE 3 DEGREES OF FREEDOM

THESE ARE THE SCORES YOU ENTERED FOR X.

1 = 2
2 = 4
3 = 4
4 = 5
5 = 6

THESE ARE THE SCORES YOU ENTERED FOR Y.

1 = 6
2 = 6
3 = 7
4 = 8
5 = 9

EX = 21

EY = 36

$EX^2 = 97$

$EY^2 = 266$

EXY = 158

N = 5

$$EXY - \frac{(EX)(EY)}{N} = 6.8$$

LOWER LEFT BRACKETS

$$EX^2 - \frac{(EX)^2}{N} = 8.8$$

LOWER RIGHT BRACKETS

$$EY^2 - \frac{(EY)^2}{N} = 6.8$$

8.8 TIMES 6.8 = 59.84

THE SQUARE ROOT OF 59.84 = 7.74

$$r = \frac{6.8}{7.74} = .88$$

DEGREES OF FREEDOM ARE

N - 2 = DF

5 - 2 = 3

THE NUMBER OF SCORES (N) IS 10.

THE MEAN OF THE SCORES ($\overline{X}$) IS 5.7.

THE SD FOR A POPULATION IS 1.95.

THE SD FOR A SAMPLE IS 2.06.

| SCORE | z-SCORE | Z OR T-SCORE |
|---|---|---|
| 2 | -1.8 | 32 |
| 4 | -.83 | 41.7 |
| 4 | -.83 | 41.7 |
| 5 | -.34 | 46.6 |
| 6 | .15 | 51.5 |
| 6 | .15 | 51.5 |
| 6 | .15 | 51.5 |
| 7 | .63 | 56.3 |
| 8 | 1.12 | 61.2 |
| 9 | 1.6 | 66 |

```
FOR THE TEST ONE VS TWO.
=================================
N OF ONE = 5
SUM OF SCORES = 21
MEAN = 4.2
SUM OF SQUARED SCORES = 103
THE 'SS' OF ONE = 14.8

N OF TWO = 5
SUM OF SCORES = 21
MEAN = 4.2
SUM OF SQUARED SCORES = 95
THE 'SS' OF TWO = 6.8

THE t VALUE IS 0
THE DEGREES OF FREEDOM ARE 8
===================================
```

THE N IS 5

THE t VALUE IS 10.1559

THERE ARE 4 DEGREES OF FREEDOM

$\bar{D} = 3.8$

$ED^2 = 75$

$ED = 19$

$N = 5$

$$\frac{ED^2 - \frac{(ED)^2}{N}}{N(N-1)} = .14$$

$$\sqrt{.14} = .3742$$

$$\frac{3.8}{.3742} = 10.1559$$

YOU ENTERED THE FOLLOWING SCORES IN

GROUP ONE:

2, 3, 4, 5, 7,

YOU ENTERED THE FOLLOWING SCORES IN

GROUP TWO:

3, 3, 4, 5, 6,

YOU ENTERED THE FOLLOWING SCORES IN

GROUP THREE:

7, 8, 8, 8, 9,

| GROUP | NO. SCORES | SUM OF SCORES | SUM OF SQUARED SCORES |
|---|---|---|---|
| ONE | 5 | 21 | 103 |
| TWO | 5 | 21 | 95 |
| THREE | 5 | 40 | 322 |

SUMS OF SCORES

$SS_T = 71.73$

$SS_B = 48.13$

$SS_W = 23.6$

| SOURCE OF VARIATION | SUM OF SQUARES | | DF | MEAN SQUARE |
|---|---|---|---|---|
| BETWEEN | 48.13 | (K-1) | 2 | 24.07 |
| WITHIN | 23.6 | (N-K) | 12 | 1.97 |
| TOTAL | 71.73 | (N-1) | 14 | F=12.24 |

SCHEFFE TESTS

| COMPARISON | F-RATIO |
|---|---|
| ONE VS TWO | 0 |
| ONE VS THREE | 9.18 |
| TWO VS THREE | 9.18 |
| ONE VS TWO & THREE | 3.06 |

$X^2$ FOR CATEGORY 1= 1.45

$X^2$ FOR CATEGORY 2= 1.45

$X^2$ FOR CATEGORY 3= 5.91

$X^2$ = 8.81

THERE ARE 2 DEGREES OF FREEDOM.

## PART NINE

## SELF-TEST FOR TASK 9

### Reading Time in School: Effect on Fourth Graders' Performance on a Criterion-Referenced Comprehension Test

### GENERAL EVALUATION CRITERIA

### Introduction

CODE

Problem

A statement? . . . . . . . . . . Y
Paragraph (//)9, sentence (S)1[1]
Researchable? . . . . . . . . . . Y
Background information? . . . . . . . . . . Y
e.g., //1, //7
Significance discussed? . . . . . . . . . . Y
e.g., //2
Variables and relationships discussed? . . . . . . . . . . Y
Definitions? . . . . . . . . . . N
Apparently assumes common knowledge of terms such as criterion-referenced test

Review of Related Literature

Comprehensive? . . . . . . . . . . ?/X
Appears to be
References relevant? . . . . . . . . . . Y
Sources primary? . . . . . . . . . . Y
Critical analysis? . . . . . . . . . . Y
e.g., //4-6
Well organized? . . . . . . . . . . Y
Summary? . . . . . . . . . . N
Rationale for hypotheses? . . . . . . . . . . NA
There are no hypotheses

Hypotheses

Questions or hypotheses? . . . . . . . . . . N
Expected differences stated? . . . . . . . . . . NA
Variables defined? . . . . . . . . . . NA
Testable? . . . . . . . . . . NA
Note. Since the answer to the first question is N, the remainder of the questions become NA.

---

[1](//)9 refers to paragraph 9 of the introduction section of the article. The introduction section ends where Procedure begins.

## Method

CODE

Subjects

| | |
|---|---|
| Population described? | N |
| Sample selection method described? | N |
| Selection method "good"? | ?/X |
| Avoidance of volunteers? | ?/X |
| Sample described? | Y |
| //1, S1 & 6 | |
| Minimum sizes? | Y |
| $n_1$= 20; $n_2$= 21; $n_3$= 20 | |

Instruments

| | |
|---|---|
| Rationale for selection? | NA |
| the CTBS was given before the study began; the SCST was developed for the study | |
| Instruments described? | N & Y |
| CTBS, no; SCST, yes | |
| Appropriate? Y | |
| Evidence that the SCST is appropriate for sample? | Y[2] |
| Validity discussed? | Y |
| Reliability discussed? | Y |
| Subtest reliabilities? | Y |
| Procedures for development described? | Y |
| Administration, scoring, and interpretation procedures described? | N |

Design and Procedure

| | |
|---|---|
| Design appropriate? | Y |
| Procedures sufficiently detailed? | Y |
| Pilot study described? | NA |
| Control procedures described? | Y |
| e.g., //13 | |
| Confounding variables discussed? | N |

## Results

| | |
|---|---|
| Appropriate descriptive statistics? | Y |
| Probability level specified in advance? | N |
| Parametric assumptions not violated? | Y |
| Tests of significance appropriate? | ?/X |
| Every hypothesis tested? | NA |
| Appropriate degrees of freedom? | ?/X |
| Results clearly presented? | Y |
| Tables well organized? | Y |
| There are no figures | |
| Data in each table described? | Y |

---

[2]The CTBS is a well-known, valid and reliable test battery.

## Discussion (Conclusions and Recommendations)

| | CODE |
|---|---|
| Results discussed in terms of hypotheses? But they are discussed in terms of the problem statement. | NA |
| Results discussed in terms of previous research? e.g., //2, last sentence | Y |
| Generalizations consistent with results? e.g., //2 | Y |
| Effects of uncontrolled variables discussed? | N |
| Implications discussed? | Y |
| Recommendations for action? e.g., //6, S2 | Y |
| Suggestions based on practical significance? | Y |
| Recommendations for research? Recommendation is general (//6, S5) | Y & N |

## Abstract (or Summary)

| | |
|---|---|
| Problem restated? | Y |
| Subjects and instruments described? | Y |
| Design identified? | N |
| Procedures? | Y |
| Results and conclusions? | Y |

## METHOD-SPECIFIC EVALUATION CRITERIA

Design used:

A pretest-posttest control group design, with each group serving as a comparison (control) group for the others.

Subjects were randomly assigned to treatments.

The independent variable was amount of reading time.

R O $X_1$ O
R O $X_2$ O
R O $X_3$ O

$X_1$ = reading only
$X_2$ = reading/skill instruction
$X_3$ = skill instruction only

O = SCST scores

CODE

|  | Code |
|---|---|
| Design appropriate? | Y |
| Design selection rationale? Not directly | N |
| Invalidity discussed? | N |
| Group formation described? | Y |
| Groups formed in same way? | Y |
| Groups randomly formed? | Y |
| Treatments randomly assigned? | N |
| Extraneous variables described? e.g., under Experimental Procedures, last sentence. | Y |
| Groups equated? Analysis of covariance was used; pretest scores served as the covariate. | Y |
| Reactive arrangements controlled for? | N |